ב"ה

A MEMENTO FROM THE

NATIONAL JEWISH RETREAT

JW MARRIOTT RESORT & SPA
PALM SPRINGS, CA 2023

NATIONAL
JEWISH
RETREAT

FIRST PRINTING
January 2022

David Green
Cover Design and Illustrations: David Green
Graphic Design and Layout: www.chayamurik.com
Photography: Moshe Schlass

For additional copies and speaking arrangements
david@realyouproject.com
www.realyouproject.com

ISBN: 978-1-61465-933-4

PICTURES OF YOUR SOUL

DAVID GREEN

Ktav Publishing House
527 Empire Blvd
Brooklyn, NY 11225
718-972-5449

Distributed by:
Menucha Publishers, Inc.
1235 38th Street
Brooklyn, NY 11218
Tel/Fax: 718-232-0856
sales@menuchapublishers.com
www.menuchapublishers.com

In loving memory of

JOYCE GREEN Z"L

MARCH 8, 1933 – AUGUST 10, 2020

REGAL, LOVING AND WISE.

Thank you

JOSH GABAY

for our inspirational nightly learning of Tanya. You lit up the path every step of the way.

ABOUT THE AUTHOR

RABBI DAVID GREEN

David Green is the Author of ***"A Book About You"*** and director of the ***Real You Project***. He studied music composition in IU Bloomington and has been recording and composing for decades. He has worked with some of the most famous names in music and is an award-winning film producer...winner of the Cable Ace Award for his film Deadly Currents and the Health and Medical Film festival for his movie Home Safe, distributed by Disney. As an inventor, he serves as CEO of Edensoles ltd. David received Rabbinic Ordination at the Mir yeshiva and has been teaching and counseling in various educational programs for over 30 years. David is a renowned international teacher, speaker, and performer. He now lives with his wife and children in Israel.

ABOUT THE PHOTOGRAPHER

MOSHE SCHLASS

Rabbi Moshe Schlass is a seasoned photographer in Jerusalem, Israel. His dynamic personality and empathy shine in all his works. Born in Poland in 1939, he went through the deportation camps and landed by miracle in New York, USA, in 1949. Moshe has traveled extensively around the world, including France, Spain, Italy, Sweden, Germany, Russia, Algeria, Poland, Tunisia and many more.

In 1978, Moshe moved to Jerusalem and opened up a Chabad house in the Old City. With the help of his wife, Leah, he has hosted and fed tens of thousands of people from all around the globe! In 2008, a guest offered him a free camera, and this was the beginning of a beautiful and inspirational journey seeing only good from behind the lens.

Moshe spends four to five hours a day, six days a week at the Western Wall, connecting and interacting, taking photos of people at the Wall that unites us all.

"Some people love written text, others enjoy the visual. Combining the two in one book is artistic but hardly unique.

What makes this book special is the combination of Tanya concepts and artistic photos. Profound ideas and sacred text presented in both mediums."

RABBI MANIS FRIEDMAN

WORLD-RENOWNED AUTHOR, COUNSELOR, LECTURER AND PHILOSOPHER

Congregation Aish Kodesh
of Woodmere
351 Midwood Road
Woodmere, N. Y. 11598
516 - 569-2660

RABBI MOSHE WEINBERGER

קהילת אש קודש דוודמיר

הרב משה וויינבערגער
מרא דאתרא

ב"ה

חנוכה תשפ"ב

It is well known that the words "תא שמע," "come and listen" are the Talmud's invitation to engage in the analysis of a new explanation of halacha, a resolution of a legal dilemma or debate. The Zohar, however, introduces a new teaching with "תא חזי" – "come and see." The hidden light of Torah cannot be fully absorbed by means of a lecture or a lesson. It must be "seen," envisioned, and to whatever measure possible, experienced. Imagination and imagery lie at the core of the prophetic spirit and are invaluable tools in the art of holy meditation – התבוננות.

In "Pictures of Your Soul," David Green has wielded his mighty pen and camera to produce a masterful work of art and spirituality. Profound teachings of Chassidus come to life through David's lens, and the images convey a powerful הרגש of holiness. This is a unique sefer, one to be studied and seen, over and over again.

[illegible]

[illegible]

RABBI YAACOV HABER
Rav, Kehillas Shivtei Yeshurun
Nachal Yaaleh 7
Ramat Beit Shemesh, Israel

הרב יעקב העבר
מרא דאתרא, קהילת שבטי ישורון
רמת בית שמש

בס״ד

Teves 5752

The mark of a truly talented teacher is the ability to take complex and very sophisticated material and present it with clarity. When this is accomplished, the student not only understands the concept being taught, but will internalize the ideas forever.

Indeed, Moshe Rabbeinu himself was able to articulate an infinite light of God and convey them into words that are eternal. To do this one must not only have an exceptional power of presentation but a comprehensive understanding which is both complete and true.

My friend, R' Dovid Green, is such a teacher. By combining years of study and contemplation of complex ideas, and a world class ability to present them, he has produced a work with lessons that will live eternally within the reader. I can hardly wait to share this with my own students.

With admiration and love,

Rabbi Yaacov Haber

US: 212 561 5131 Israel: -972 52 539 5216 rabbiyhaber@gmail.com

TABLE OF CONTENTS

YOU ARE WALKING IN THE FOREST

You're walking through a forest, a gentle breeze pleasantly brushing your face. Birds are chirping over the sound of a flowing stream beside you. As you walk, you feel calm and free and peaceful. The longer you walk through the trees, the wind rustling the leaves, the city and the distractions of your life are receding further and further behind you into a distant, other world. You are now far from the hectic city and distractions of your phone and usual busy environment. Gradually, you are feeling more awake and alive, in tune and at one with your surroundings. The longer you walk through the trees, listening to birdsong, the more you have transcended into another state of being, to a feeling of connection to something both within you and beyond you. More than just a fleeting emotional boost of happiness or relaxation, you are experiencing your soul, your unique spark, an intimacy with the real you.

We constantly refer to the soul in expressions like "soul searching," "soul music," "soul sisters," body and soul," "heart and soul," "lost soul," "bless my soul," even "soul food." We speak of someone as having a soulful expression. Shakespeare is replete with references to the soul, as in "Love does not see with eyes but with the soul," but most often, it's just a vague reference to some mysterious entity, to something we assume that we can't really know, understand or even articulate. How strange it is, then, that this "entity," which all of us possess and which is so vitally crucial and to which we refer so often, should be so mysterious?

But shouldn't the path that delights our soul be the one that influences our life choices and experiences?

Although the word "soul" is such a staple of everyday speech, contemporary western culture has increasingly minimized the existence and importance of spirituality. Living in a world dominated by pragmatic, quantitative thinking and values results in an emphasis on the immediate gratification and verifiable experience at the expense of what is far more important and essential for our well-being. Biblically speaking, we have forgotten that we do not live by bread alone and have become oblivious to the fact that we must nourish the soul. And the natural byproduct of living in a world dominated by such thinking is that this awareness rarely informs our consciousness.

But shouldn't the path that delights our soul be the one that influences our life choices and experiences? The effort to learn about our soul—who we really are and how to fulfill our potential—is what ideally should take precedence and become our priority, even as we deal with our commitments and responsibilities. Perhaps that is why so many people, consciously or subconsciously, escape the routine of their lives to take a journey to get in touch with their soul. Some turn to meditation and prayer, others head to the mountains and mystics of the Far East, hoping to feel inspiration through meditation and experiencing the beauty of God's creation. There are those, given the constraints of their everyday lives, who choose less dramatic measures, finding their soul connection through an uplifting piece of music. Others just close their eyes and feel themselves connected to the people—the souls—around them. Increasingly, more people have been looking into the Jewish sources to learn what they say about waking up to our souls, where there is a rich reservoir of wisdom on the topic.

The more I learned, the more I achieved inner peace.

I believe that for years, I was searching for something deep inside me, but until my early twenties, I had no idea what it was. After years of chasing success as a musician, adrift in the confusion of trying to be unique, a number of disquieting questions and longings led me on my path to Israel, where I studied in Yeshiva. The more I learned, the more I achieved inner peace. I was exposed to an incredible source of wisdom that helped me get more in touch with my soul. So many of the philosophical questions that had troubled me about who I was and what I was were finally being addressed by teachers, experiences and the wealth of knowledge in our own Jewish texts. My music flourished as I became more and more in touch with the source of my music, my inner self and my soul.

In time, like many artists, I became more and more interested in Chassidic and Kabbalistic teachings. Remarkably, I discovered we have thousands of years of wisdom to help us understand and maximize our ongoing awareness and elevation of the soul. I hope to share with you some of the key points that continue to help me on my ongoing personal path to spiritual awareness.

Music continues to be a powerful means to connect to my inner self, and I have made a point of writing songs that express my journey. Most of the songs from my album *Journey to the Real You* were shared in my first book, *A Book About You, Individuality and Soul Awareness*. I have since recorded a new album. Please take a listen on my website, www.realyouproject.com/music. A song describing my personal path to self-discovery is entitled "Long Journey." Here are the lyrics to the first verse and chorus.

LONG JOURNEY

Yearning inspiration
Behind the blinds of many
minds and nations
Stretched my imagination
Find a place to make my own

Too many destinations
Tried to hard to fake my acclamation
I hear my inclination
I'm just longing for a place called home

Long Journey
Long Journey
You finally returned me to
the place I've been yearning
Long Journey
It's a long, long journey home

WWW.REALYOUPROJECT.COM/LJ

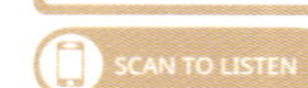

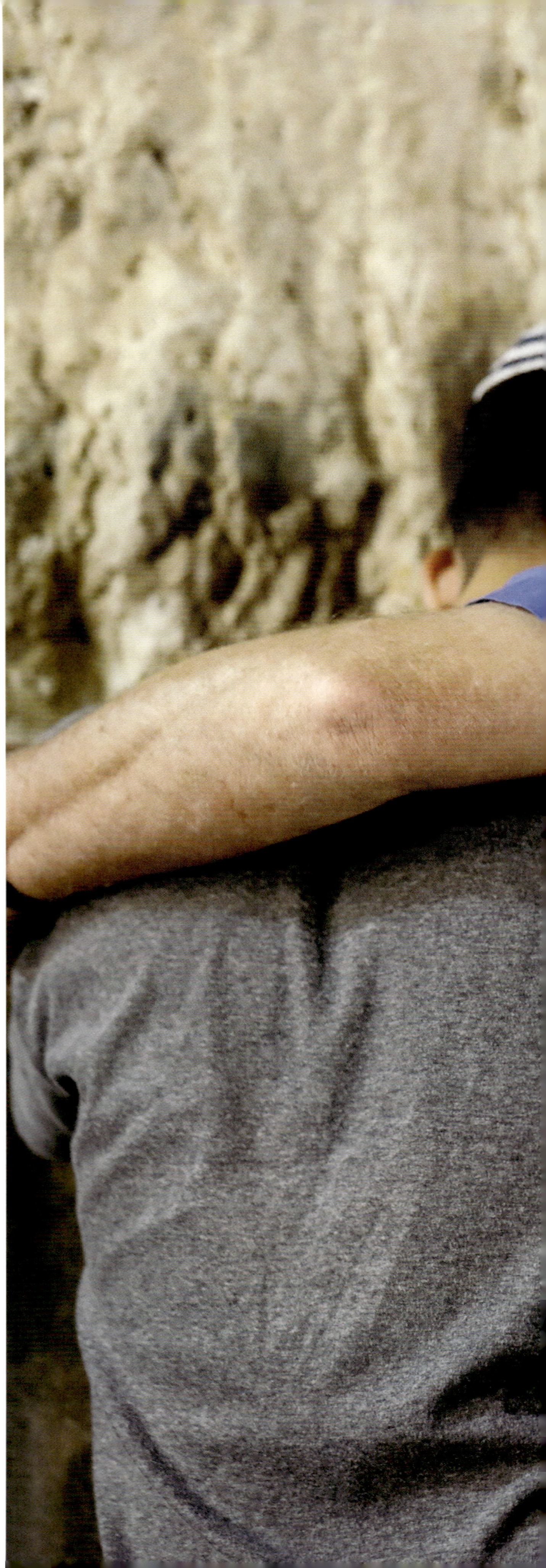

A REAL SELFIE

Today, everyone is taking selfies. But what do they really see besides their external selves? Although you can't physically see your soul, Jewish sources through the ages have given us insights into the soul and its spiritual anatomy. Hopefully, these pages will communicate these insights with images that portray the aspects of your soul. Many Jewish sources discuss its spiritual components and help us to understand and envision how these components function independently and interact with each other.

These visualizations and connections will allow you to become intimately familiar with your soul.

These visualizations and connections will allow you to become intimately familiar with your soul. It is important to keep in mind that these visualizations portray a template (i.e., components that each of us shares), but your soul is unique, unlike any other. Although our souls all share the same basic components, each is unique. Just as no two blades of grass or snowflakes are identical, how much more so is this true of human beings.

When studying the kabbalistic (Jewish mystical) sources describing the anatomy of the soul, I found it helpful to grasp the abstract concepts by actually drawing diagrams to help me integrate and visualize what I was learning. The sophisticated designs and spiritual formations discussed in these sources became so much more tangible by drawing clear images to help me follow the text. So, although we cannot literally see the soul the way we can x-ray parts of the body, these sources, extrapolating from the Torah, allow us to form images helping us to conceptualize connections, processes, and interactions between the components of the soul.

So, together, let's explore the anatomy of your soul for the purpose of helping you achieve greater spiritual growth. Let's use the images to help you connect to the most essential part of who you are. As you can see by the format, I have structured this book around a series of questions that should perturb us when exploring the soul. I hope your questions will also be answered.

In addition to the illustrations, *Pictures of Your Soul* has been embellished by a number of beautiful photographs taken by Moshe Schlass at the Kotel (Western Wall) in Jerusalem. Each picture has been carefully chosen to enhance the message of the text by allowing us to look deep into the eyes and souls of people while they are on fire with spiritual inspiration. I'm sure you will find them uplifting.

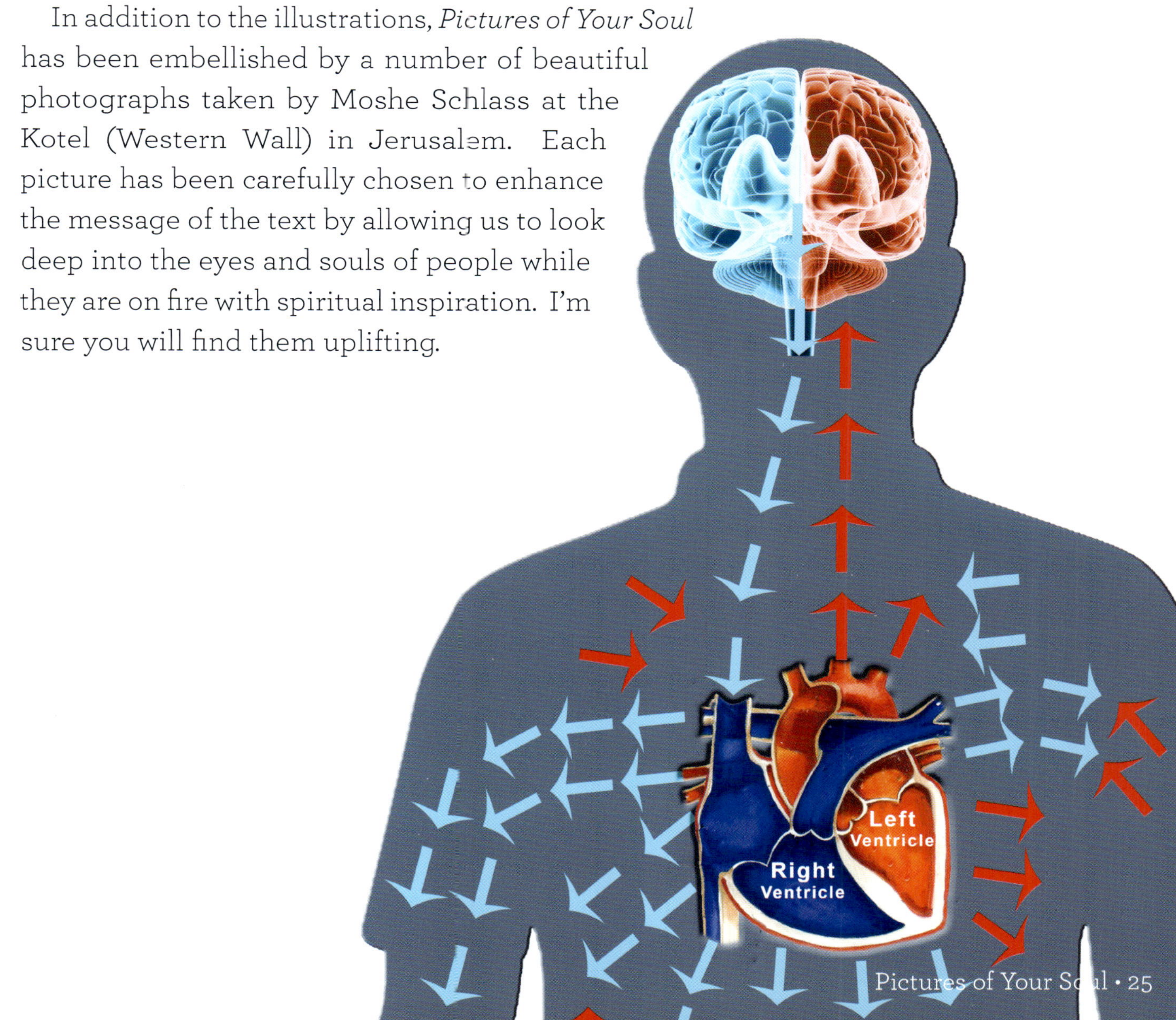

URCES

There are many kabbalistic and Chassidic works that discuss the depths of the soul. For the purpose of clarity, I have chosen a few of the most well-referenced primary sources. Among them are the *Tanya*, Zohar, the Arizal, *Nefesh Hachaim* and the Ramchal. These are sources that deal with the anatomy of the soul, in addition to delving deeply into understanding how to serve God on a very high level and using the formidable challenges of life to achieve spiritual growth. We will concentrate on those sections that deal more directly with the definition, description and functionality of the soul, as well as how to use this awareness for our personal growth.

One of the fundamental difficulties of a project like this is that it is essentially endless; many fundamental sources deal with our topic, and each topic includes numerous issues filling not only a book of many pages but also several volumes written over thousands of years. It has been a challenge to both avoid being simplistic and not be so complex as to confound my readers. So, at the outsell, I am issuing the caveat that the enclosed intends only to provide you with a meaningful introduction to the subject of your soul and what I have discerned based on my determinations. Hopefully, these pages will inspire you to further explore the topic of your soul.

Much of this book is based more on *Tanya* which is

a classic work by Rabbi Shneur Zalman of Liadi, first published in 1797. It is composed of five sections that define Chassidic mystical psychology and theology as a handbook for daily spiritual life in Jewish observance.

Although I use the *Tanya* more than the other named sources to explain the soul, I did not intend to explore the entire *Tanya* and related chapters on this topic. I have structured the format to address those commonly asked questions about the soul, using the *Tanya* as my major reference. The questions that comprise the format were formulated to provide a comprehensive picture of your living soul—its anatomy, its goals, its challenges, its every present connection between our physical selves and God—as we make those life choices that determine the quality of our lives. There are countless sources, many of them classics, that deal with the soul, but concentrating primarily on the *Tanya* has helped me and hopefully you, the reader, to navigate the complexity of this topic.

אין כניסה
כניסה

THE BIG PICTURE

WHERE IS MY SOUL?

We all sense that there is something intangible within us besides just our physical organs. We sense that it is both connected to us yet separate. It fills the inner space of our bodies, and yet it is totally spiritual, so it won't show up on an x-ray, a CAT scan or an MRI. It is that living force within us that is the essence of our being. Paradoxically, what is most important and authentic about us is that which is most invisible and amorphous. Here is a powerful analogy that should help us identify more with the nature of our soul.

The soul (*Neshama*) of man is a candle of God.[1] The human soul is like a flame connected to a candle by a wick, always reaching upwards. Ironically, if the flame were to rise above the wick, it would be extinguished. So too your soul, although connected to your body, constantly rises up to return to its source out of its natural love for its creator. But our souls remain connected to our bodies so they can serve their purpose of helping us lead a spiritually meaningful life in this world. The body is like a tool for the soul to express itself and bring spirituality within the physical realm. So let's try to acquaint you with your soul so you will feel a more intimate connection to your inner self, develop a more effective way of thinking that will have a positive impact in all areas of your life and ultimately experience a deeper connection to God. Your soul awareness will thus factor into many of your critical life choices since it is the most essential part of who you really are.

1 Mishlei 20:27

God is constantly doing the same thing by breathing your soul into you, keeping you alive every moment.

HOW DID I GET MY SOUL?

The Torah describes a process of God breathing life into the first man through his nostrils. Not only was this how the soul was originally given to us, but it is a constant process keeping us alive every moment, both physically and spiritually. We must appreciate that we were not created and then put into autopilot but constantly enlivened; although breathing is a process we are most often unconscious of, every breath is a fresh new gift of life that should never be taken for granted.

In the Zohar,1 we find "the Nefesh level of the soul is bound to the *Ruach*, the Ruach to the Neshama, and the Neshama to the Blessed Holy One." The three thus form a chain-like continuum, linking man to God. The idea of these three parts is best explained on the basis of the verse, "God formed man out of the dust of the earth, and He blew into his nostrils a breath of life."2 This can be compared to the process of blowing glass, which begins with the breath (*Neshima*) of the glassblower. He blows a wind (Ruach) through the glassblowing pipe, and it finally comes to rest (*Nefesh*) in the vessel that is being formed. The Neshama thus comes from the same root as Neshima, meaning breath, and this is the "breath of God." The meaning of the word Nefesh is "to rest" and therefore refers to the part of the soul that is bound to the body and "rests" there. Ruach means a wind, and it is the part of the soul that binds the Neshama to the Nefesh.[3]

Here is a miniature version of a meditation to help us climb up through the levels of the soul. Try sitting still and concentrating on your breathing. For a few minutes, slowly inhale through your nose, hold it in and slowly exhale. Become aware of your breathing as well as a spiritual connection to your head, heart and liver or stomach. Practicing such a meditation will help you become more aware of your Nefesh, Ruach and Neshama. On a Divine level, God is constantly doing the same thing by breathing your soul into you, keeping you alive every moment, physically and spiritually.

---

1 Zohar III:25a

2 Gen. 2:7

3 *Nefesh Hachaim* 1:15

DOES MY SOUL HAVE PARTS?

Although the soul is unified, it is also divided into different parts. Depending on the angle with which we look at the soul, different divisions will appear. From a broad angle, or wide perspective, it is divided into five parts, Nefesh, Ruach, Neshama, *Chaya* and *Yechida*. From a closer view, it is very common to refer, as stated above, only to the bottom three levels since they are referred to as *pnimim*,[1] which means that they reside within the body, while Chaya and Yechida hover above. Chaya means "the living one" and is the place of our consciousness, while Yechida means "oneness" and is connected to God's unity.

The lowest level of the soul is housed in the blood of a human being, giving life to the body, "For the Nefesh of the flesh is in the blood."[2] The Nefesh is the contact point found within the blood that serves as a connection to the higher levels of the soul all the way up to the level of Yechida. Close your eyes and simply feel your soul and its connection to the blood as it flows throughout your inner space. Starting with your feet, feel the life in every part of your body as you climb up to your head, where you should feel it the most. Figuratively, we also learn that the Neshama level is located in the brain, Ruach in the heart and Nefesh in the liver.

---

1 Breishis Raba 54:9

2 Vayikra 17:11

Yechida
Chaya
Neshama
Ruach
Nefesh

HOW DOES MY SOUL STAY WITHIN MY PHYSICAL BODY?

It is experientially obvious that our souls are connected to our bodies. I can recall so many times in my life, since I was a kid, where I felt something within me that was on fire. I was so inspired that I forgot all about where I was physically while I was totally tuned into something so much more ethereal and spiritual. I could be playing music, listening to an amazing concert, focusing on the crackling flames of a bonfire and even lying down on the ground and feeling my body as part of the greater earth and all of creation. Even more so, I have experienced this inner awakening in Jewish life from the uplifting songs at the third meal on Shabbat or from singing inspirational songs in a pitch-black room full of Chassidim. As in this picture, looking in the eyes of someone who is spiritually on fire can also be a powerful source of personal inspiration.

But the question of how the soul stays within the body is a mysteriously complex

kabbalistic topic that can be discussed for years to get even a glimpse of true understanding. It parallels the equally complex question of how God, who is infinite, can also exist within our physical world. This process is referred to as *Tzimtzum* (contraction), and its study, which we will later discuss in greater depth, is primarily focused on the initial step of transformation from God's infinite light to something that is contracted to be tangible or accessible enough for us to experience it in this world. But for now, we will focus more on the point of connection between the body and soul.

As described earlier, the levels of the soul are like a chain, Nefesh being the lowest level and therefore the closest part of the soul to the physical body. The blood, too, has levels extending from very physical to the much more ethereal. All within the Nefesh, the most ethereal level of the blood is the meeting point between the body and soul. Since the higher levels of the soul are also connected to the Nefesh, they, too, are linked through an ongoing connection to the blood flowing through our bodies.[1]

Another way to understand the connection between the body and soul is through our glassblower analogy. Since God is constantly blowing our soul into us from the Neshama, through the Ruach and then to the Nefesh, the soul remains constantly alive and connected to our body. This is not another method. Both approaches work together being that they both describe the chain connecting the Neshama down to the Ruach and then to the Nefesh within our blood.

---

1 *Derech Hashem* (translated by Arieh Kaplan)

A CLOSER LOOK

IF MY SOUL IS HOLY, WHY DO I HAVE UNHOLY DESIRES?

TWO SOULS

Although we refer to our soul in the singular, in truth we have two spiritual life forces, the animal soul and the Divine soul, within us motivated by very different drives and spiritual aspirations. As is written, "And *Neshamot* (souls) which I have made."[1]

THE ANIMAL SOUL – NEFESH BEHAMIT

The animal soul is driven primarily toward impure, negative drives. Its source is called *Klipa*, which is like a translucent shell or peel which conceals Godliness in this world. Having both souls enables us to have free will to choose to do good or bad. This is the normal state with which mankind was created. A person shouldn't feel surprised or spiritually inferior by the fact that he/she has desires that are contrary to God's will. That is an essential part of what makes us human. If it were not for the animal soul, man would only do good and therefore be like a robot with no life of his/her own, no spiritual growth, no accomplishment and without any possibility of a meaningful, elevating relationship with God. Although we will be describing the various negative attributes of the animal soul, it is critical to keep in mind that it is ultimately a great source of life within us. The animal soul "animates" the body with the will to survive and satisfy our basic physical needs, which, if harnessed properly, serves as a powerful source of life and a vigorous force to take care of our essential needs.

Although the animal soul is full of negative drives, we must keep in mind that it is ultimately working for you to allow you to

1 Yeshayahu 57:16. (*Arizal*, *Tanya* ch.1)

TWO SOULS

pass its various tests and thereby make you a stronger person, receive the reward for your achievement and prepare you to climb to a higher spiritual level. A powerful analogy to illustrate this point is as follows: There was a king who wanted to prepare his son to be a prince. He had to make sure that he was strong enough in his own self-control to be considered prepared enough to face the world outside the palace. The king, therefore, hired a harlot to try to seduce him. It was the wish of the king that his dear son would be strong enough to resist this beautiful woman. Fascinatingly, it was also the wish of the harlot that the son would not succumb to her seduction. She was a messenger of the king and wanted the best results for him, so although she was hired to tempt the prince, ultimately, she was hoping to be defeated. The same applies to the animal soul. God, the ultimate king, sends the animal soul to tempt us with all kinds of forbidden pleasure, but in truth, the animal soul is ultimately on our team, hoping that we win the battle.

We must try to always remember that the Divine essence of who we are is purely holy.

THE DIVINE SOUL – NEFESH ELOKIT

As an introduction, it is critical to know that the *Nefesh Elokit,* Divine soul, is pure and only good. The *Tanya* refers to it as "a piece of God." Regardless of how we behave, the Divine soul remains pure. Just as when man blows out air, it comes from his innermost self, so too with the creation of our soul. As we quoted above, the Torah states, "And the Lord God formed man of the dust of the ground, and breathed into his nostrils the breath of life; and man became a living soul."[2] We must try to always remember that the Divine essence of who we are is purely holy. This awareness has a profound influence on how we see ourselves and how high we can climb the ladder of spiritual awareness and other areas of accomplishment. We will soon be looking deeper into the intricate design and function of the Divine soul, but first, let's get a closer picture of the animal soul.

2 Bereshit 2:7

WHAT IS THE ANATOMY OF THE ANIMAL SOUL?

The klipa of the animal soul is created through the channels of confusion and negativity that God created called *Sitra Achra,* which means "the other side"—the side of creation that is the antithesis of holiness and purity. The Sitra Achra is part of the bigger picture of good and evil that has filled the world since the original sin. Negative drives and behavior and overall impurity derive their vitality from this Sitra Achra. Although everything is created by God, who is all good, His world contains an aspect of creation, which is impure, operating ultimately for our benefit since our challenging choices in life provide the opportunity to elevate ourselves and the world as a whole.

It seems out of character for God to create a force that is essentially evil, but much like the animal soul, this force serves as our opportunity to serve the holy purpose of repairing the confusion brought down into the world through the original sin of Adam and Eve. Because of damage brought into the world by the Sitra Achra, so much meaning can be experienced in life through being a part of the noble cause of fixing the world, each in our own way.

Just as in the physical world there are four contrasting basic physical elements, so too the *Nefesh Behamit,* or animal soul, is made up of the same four negative characteristics, but they serve to divert us from achieving our spiritual aspirations. These four negative attributes are fire, air, water and earth. In the animal soul, they manifest as follows:

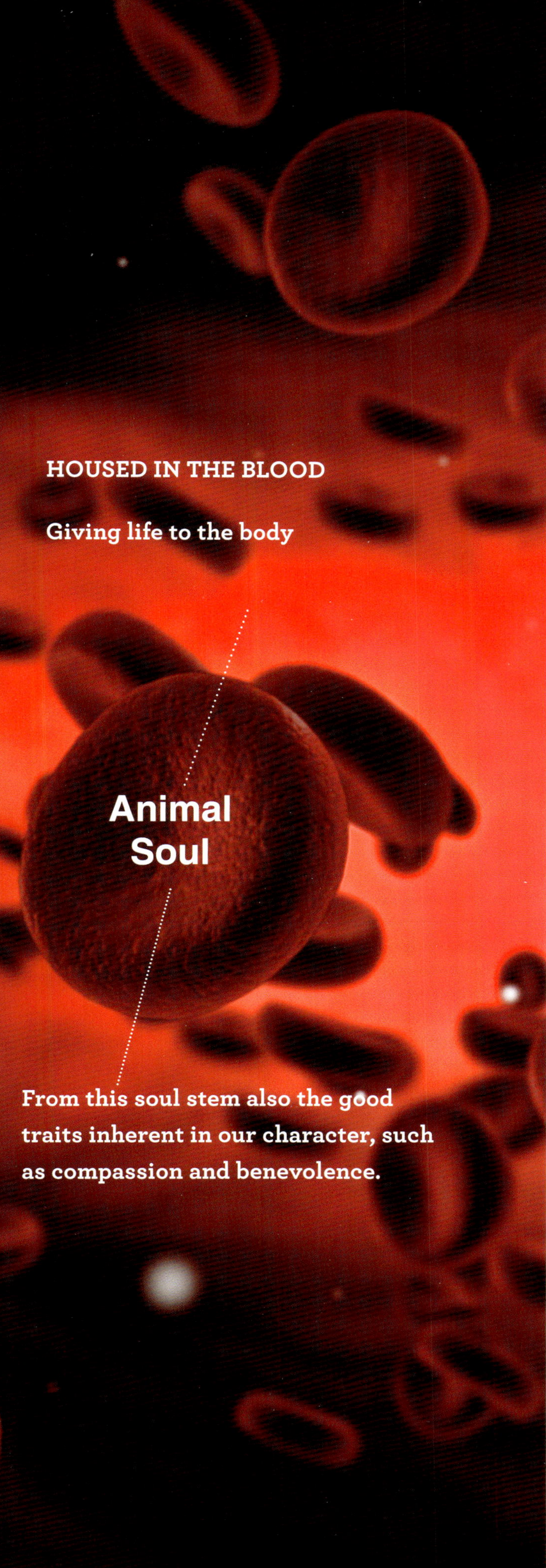

THE FOUR ELEMENTS

1. FIRE – Anger and pride
2. AIR – Frivolity, scoffing, boasting and idle talk
3. WATER – Physical desires
4. EARTH – Laziness

These four elements can also be used by the Divine soul to express positive characteristics and actions, such as being altruistic, taking care of one's self and building self-esteem. The attribute of fire can also be expressed as a passion for serving God. The attribute of air can be expressed as the ability to transcend material desires. However, in the animal soul, these attributes are motivated by self-gratification, while when utilized by the Divine soul, they are expressed selflessly in our service of God.

In addition to the four elements, from a different angle, we find three totally impure *Klipot*, each being purely negative, empty of any goodness whatsoever. There is another level of the animal soul called *Klipat Noga*, which has a mixture of good and bad and serves as a source of confusing the two. This means that on the one hand, it serves as a covering of Godliness, but if we use our strength, clarity of thought and strong will, Klipat Noga can also be harnessed to be used for good. Let's take a closer look at Klipat Noga.

KLIPAT NOGA

As briefly mentioned above, the origin of Klipat Noga is an expression of the tree of knowledge of good and evil from which Adam and Eve ate in the Garden of Eden. The consequence of the original sin internalized the confusion of Klipat Noga, making it hard to differentiate between what is true and false, permitted and forbidden. This makes it difficult to make choices when the desires of the confusing messages of the animal soul are trying to prevent us from doing what is good.

The mixture of good and bad attributes within the Klipat Noga part of the animal soul makes it very difficult to distinguish between good and bad. Therefore, they are very vulnerable to the inner voice of confusion. Not only is it difficult to distinguish between good and bad but even when we know what is wrong, we are seduced into thinking that we are too weak to resist temptation. On the other hand, although we view the animal soul as essentially bad, by learning more about it, we can examine it deeply enough to learn its tricks and strategies and thereby gain control over it, harnessing its powerful energy to do what is good and beneficial for ourselves and others.[1] Although this is very challenging, we will soon address the wisdom of how to uncover the good found within the Klipat Noga and use it to reveal the positive traits inherent in our character.

---

1 Zohar I, 12b

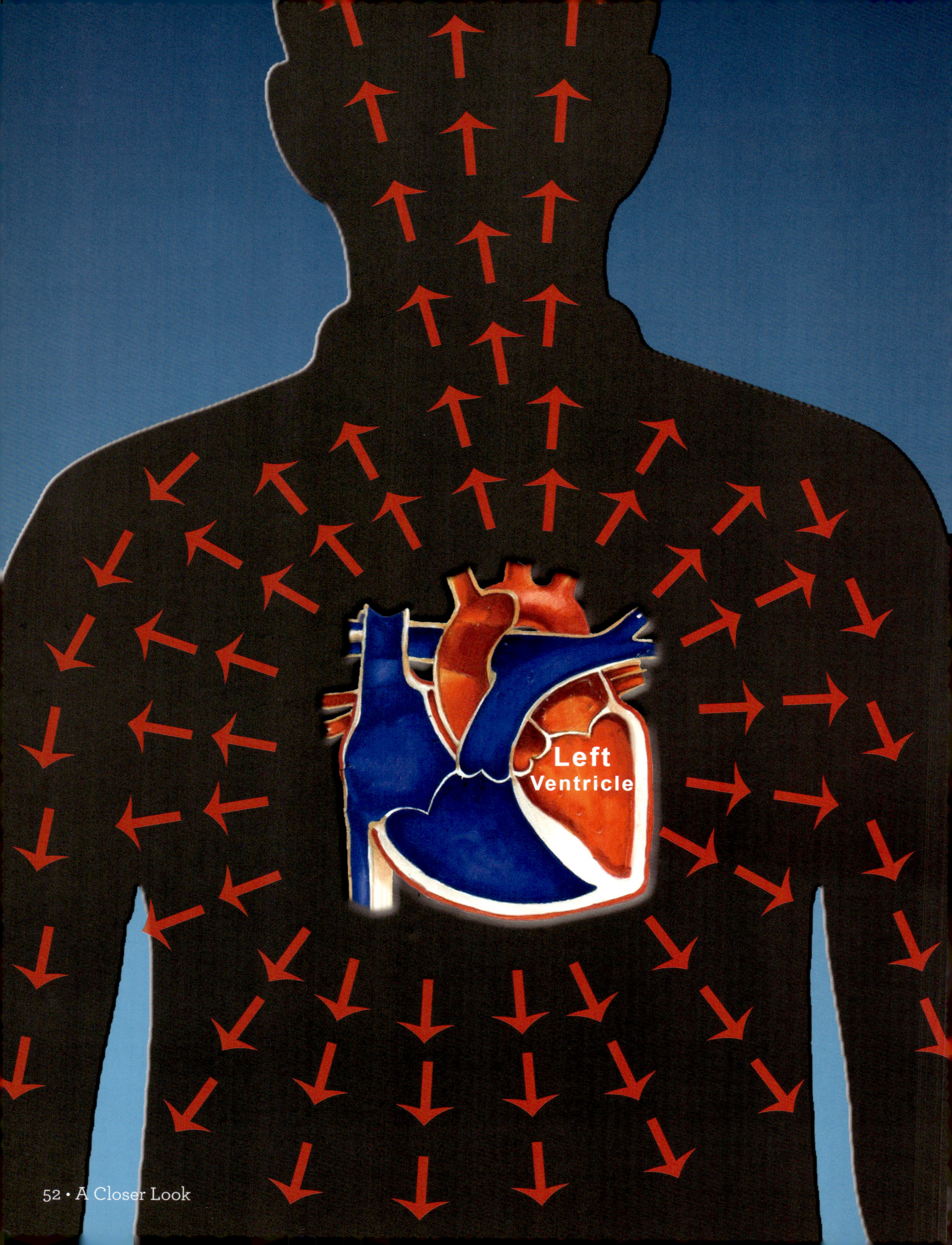
Left
Ventricle

HOW DOES MY ANIMAL SOUL IGNITE MY DESIRES?

Now let's take a closer look at the anatomy of the animal soul and how it works to control the body and our emotions. Have you ever had times when you felt a sense of calm, confident and with a strong sense of self-control? Then within a moment, everything changes, and you feel overcome by seemingly irresistible desires that were convincing you that they must be fulfilled. What happened that caused you to lose your self-confidence, self-discipline and moral dignity? Let's look at how the desires of the animal soul take control over our body and physical and material lusts.

As you can see in the picture, the left ventricle of the heart is where the blood of the animal soul is based. It continuously sends blood tainted with its negative attributes to the rest of the body, animating it with physical drives and desires as well as distorted emotional demands, such as ego, jealousy and anger. This is something we actually can feel when experiencing any of these drives. For example, when someone gets angry, you can see their blood rushing to their head and face, which is usually followed by a burst of irrational behavior, the opposite of their usual self-control and dignity.

The left ventricle of the heart is where the blood of the animal soul is based

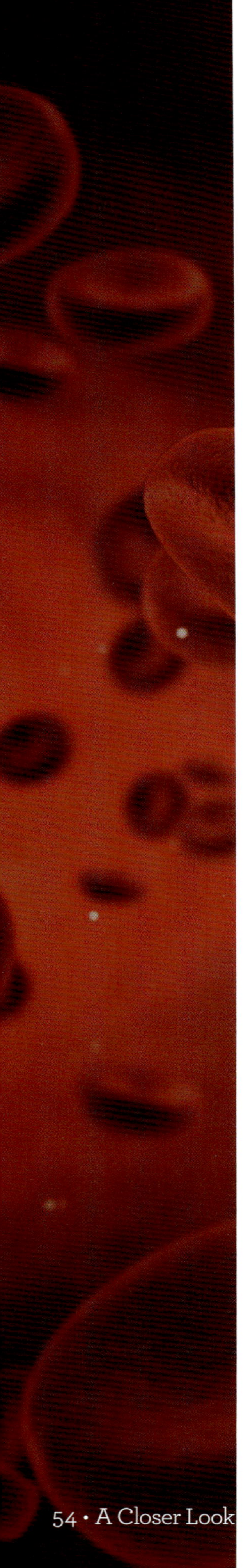

THE BLOOD OF THE ANIMAL SOUL FINDS ITS WAY TO YOUR BRAIN

where it works to confuse you into following its negative drives. Once your mind has been manipulated, polluted with convincing arguments to act upon the animal soul's desires, it is very difficult to resist. The mind is the main control center of the human body and when captured by the animal soul, its negative drives are sent back down to the body, motivating it to act in a lowly manner. Next time this happens, observe how your mind becomes a brilliant advocate for the animal soul, convincing you to follow its desires.

As we will discuss later, a mind with a clear and steadfast conviction of what is right and wrong possesses the most powerful ammunition to survive the ongoing persistent influence of the animal soul.

After a rampage of the animal soul, people usually experience regret for having lost control. This painful resentment should not be forgotten, for it can be a deterrent from allowing the animal soul to take control in the future since it is an uncomfortable feeling that even the body would prefer to avoid.

I once heard a powerful story of a man who won over his animal soul by using an anger robe. It was an amazing robe because the owner had a bad temper, but he was aware of his problem enough to come up with an effective solution. Sitting at the dinner table,

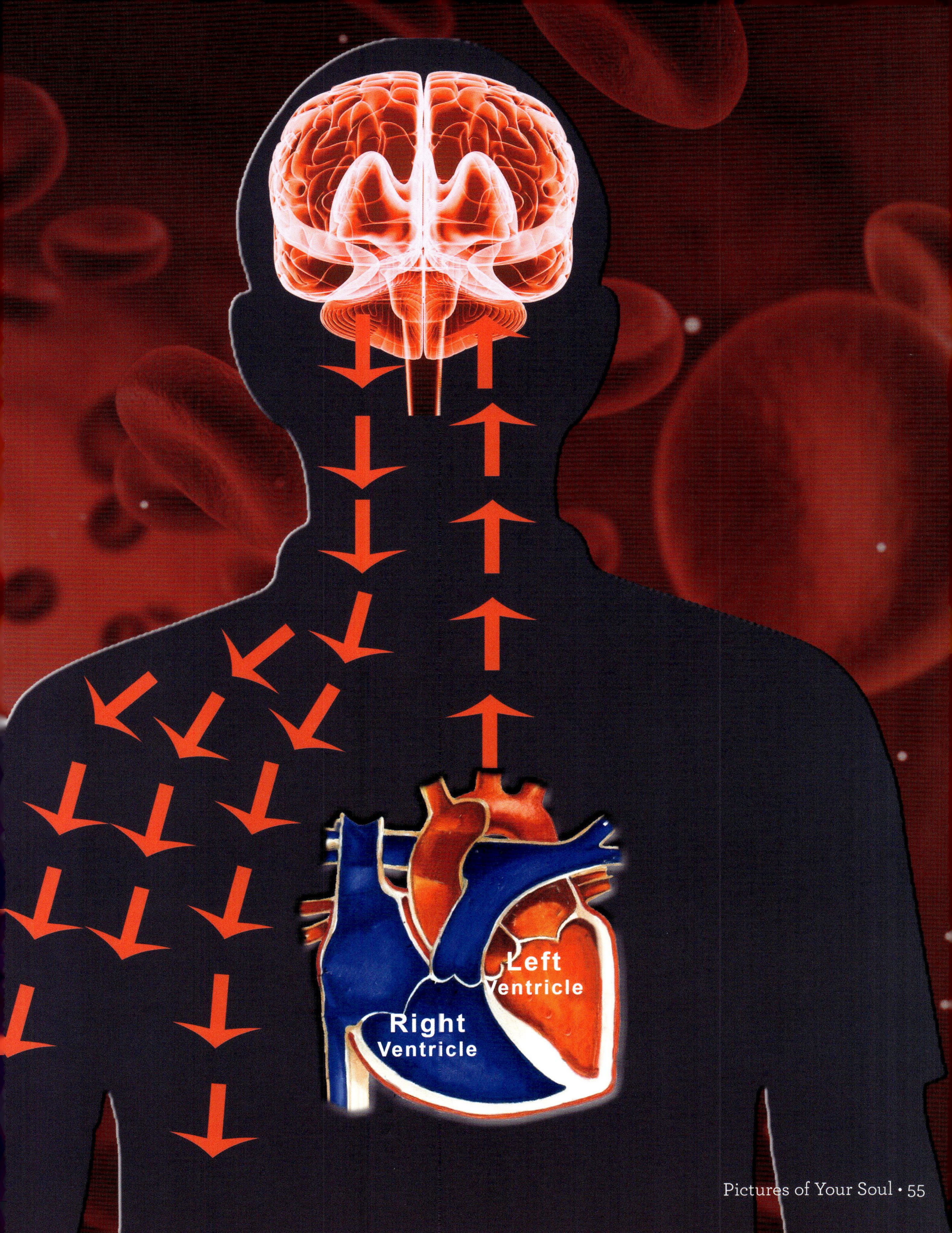
Left
Ventricle
Right
Ventricle

he frequently allowed his anger to build toward his family until he inevitably exploded with bursts of screaming uncontrollable insults, even to those whom he really loved. How embarrassing it must have been for him to look back at his lowly behavior and have to try to move forward without a deep sense of remorse and regret. After much introspection and deep soul-searching, he finally thought of a solution he called the "anger robe." This was going to solve his embarrassing outbursts. Here is how it worked: Let's return to the table with his family. Once again, he starts to get annoyed by some of the same old negative comments made by his wife. His kids pick up on the tension and start acting up, and it looks like he is going to lose it again. Time for another explosion. But this time is different. He made a brave deal with himself that he is allowed to have a temper tantrum but with one condition. He must first get up from his chair, slowly walk out of the dining room, walk up the stairs to his bedroom and then slowly make his way to his closet, where he keeps his anger robe. He then puts on the robe, ties the belt and slowly makes his way back downstairs, where he will allow himself to scream his head off. But by the time he makes it back to the table, something has changed. His blood has stopped boiling. His self-control and dignity are restored. The urge to rage has simmered, and he continues with his meal as if nothing had bothered him. What an example of transcendence! It is an important point to note that our friend had the humility to recognize that the anger was his problem, and therefore, he was halfway to the solution since he knew it was his job to come up with a solution. Humility is one of the most important qualities in the fight between our two souls. Someone in denial of their weakness will never put in the effort to overcome it.

Being able to remove yourself from the battle with your animal soul as it tries to take over your mind and body is not easy. But having a tangible strategy to allow the heat of anger to calm down gave this man, previously so controlled by his raw emotions, the ammunition to be victorious. As we learn more about how we are created, I hope you, too, will use the teachings to develop the ammunition to win your own personal battles. We all have it within us to achieve greatness, self-control and spiritual awareness.

Shortly, we will focus on the anatomy of the Divine soul and then delve into how the two souls interact with each other.

Humility is one of the most important qualities in the fight between our two souls.

DOES MY DOG HAVE A SOUL?

Yes, your dog has a soul. This is something we intuit by looking into the bright, responsive eyes of an animal. But animals differ spiritually from humans because they lack a Divine soul, which is created in the image of God. Even the animal soul of man is on a higher spiritual level than that of animals, which is evident by the fact that people can not only talk and think more intelligently but can experience a wide range of emotions and control those emotions when appropriate.

IMAGE OF GOD

"In the image of God, He created him" (Genesis 1:27)

WHAT IS THE ANATOMY OF THE DIVINE SOUL?

Now let's try to get a closer view of the Divine soul. This is the soul that is the most essential part of you. When we refer to "your soul," we are referring to the Divine soul. It is a priceless treasure whose precious value we must never forget or take for granted, especially at times when our self-image is suffering or when we have behaved dishonorably. Even at such times, we are still essentially a precious flame shining within. Regardless of where our animal soul influences us to go, we are essentially still a spark of divinity loved by God. We must do our best to always remember that if He loves us unconditionally, we have every right to love ourselves as well.

People who are unaware of the precious value and purity of the Divine soul within them have no reason to feel worthy. Too many people feel their worthiness is based on their external success. They feel their self-esteem is dependent on objective factors – for example, money or titles. Of course, achieving success is important, but it should not be the measure of who we are. We can feel proud of ourselves for performing a difficult task, making a financially wise decision, or being well-liked and sought out by others. However, the Torah view is that the Divine soul is a pure piece of Divinity which is ours regardless of any of the external signs of success. Its flame, the Divine spark, shines independently of your degrees or bank account. It is my hope that the more you become aware of the Divine soul, the easier it will be to identify with it as the most essential you and that this awareness will become life transforming.

I recently heard a story about a man who was not only asocial but also a complete introvert. He rarely received any greetings of "hello" or "how are you?" from the people who lived in his apartment building, in the elevator or even when he would walk through the park or to the local shopping market. One day, he passed by a hat store, and he was inspired to buy himself a new one. Excited by his new purchase, he decided to put his old hat in the hatbox he got from the store and wear his new hat. Strangely, as he strolled back home, he was greeted by almost everyone he saw. Little kids asked him for help crossing the street. People he regularly saw in the park all said hello and asked how he was doing. Even in the elevator up to his apartment, people cared enough to initiate conversations, as if he was their old buddy. When he arrived home, his wife asked him how he was doing. He enthusiastically pointed to his hat. Perplexed, she asked him what he meant. "My new hat. What do you think of it?" She didn't know what he was talking about, so he took off his hat and noticed that he mistakenly put his new hat in the box and wore his old hat. If one has an inner sense of value, the world around them changes, just as being aware of the piece of divinity within you can dramatically change the way you perceive yourself and the way others perceive you.

As we look deeper into the anatomy of the Divine soul, we find that besides the five levels of the soul described above, it also contains ten Godly attributes, which are each associated with parts of the human body. In order to understand the nature and source of these ten attributes, I ask for your patience as we consider a brief introduction to some basic kabbalistic principles.

Warning: Before trying to explore and understand these principles, it is critical to know that we are delving into ideas that can be easily misunderstood. The main concern is the danger of interpreting the following as implying that God has parts or is limited in some way. That is furthest from the truth. None of what we are about to explore should in any way be interpreted as implying that God is divided into parts or is not infinite and perfect. We can only understand these concepts to a limited extent because God's perfection is beyond the capacity of the human mind. So, although we are going to learn the following ideas via the teachings of the great kabbalist scholars, we should not assume we have a true and complete understanding, only a somewhat clearer picture of our soul.

Being aware of the piece of divinity within you can dramatically change the way you perceive yourself and the way others perceive you.

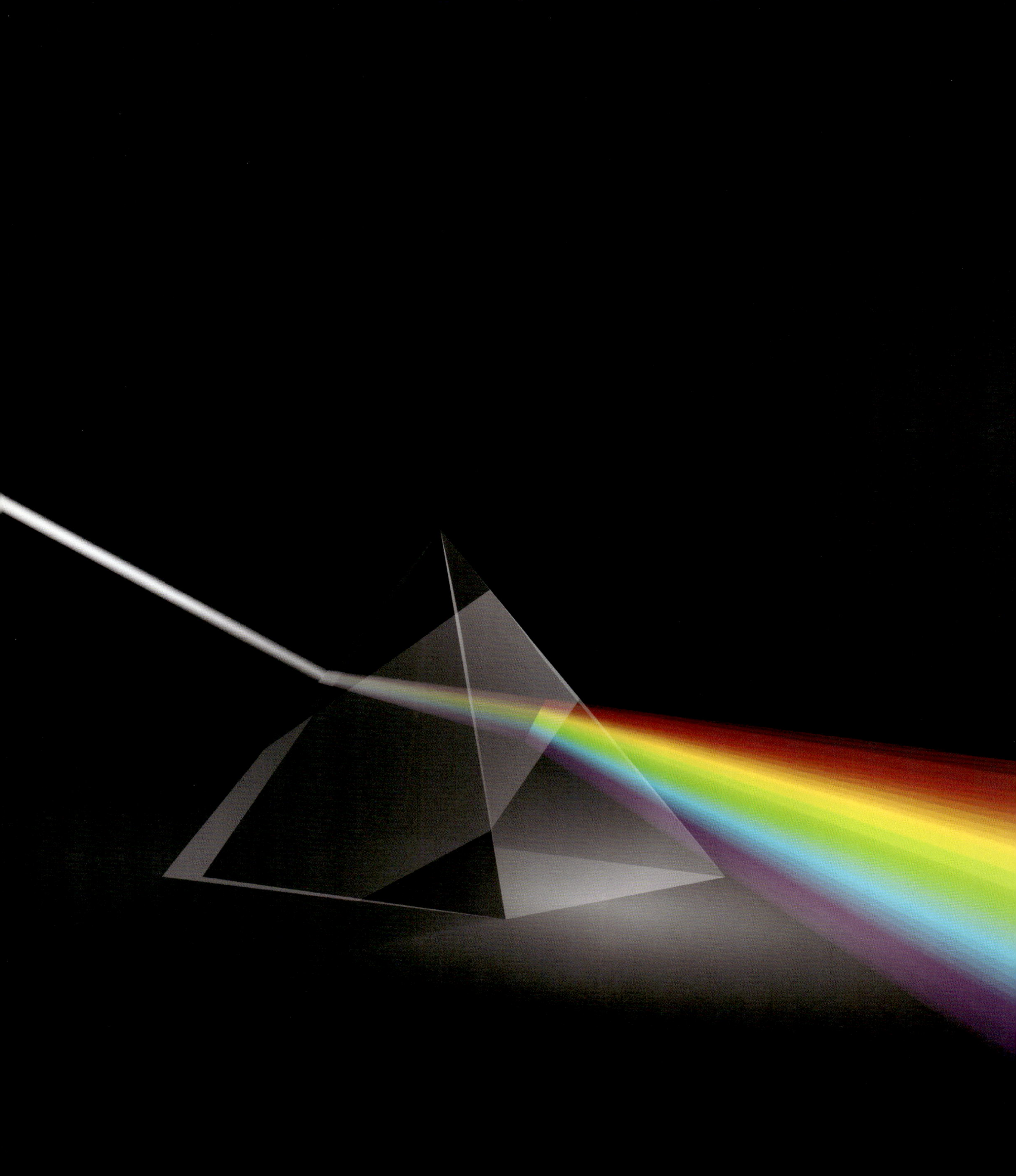

ENDLESS LIGHT

Before the creation of the world, there was only pure, infinite Godliness referred to as Ein Sof. When creating the world, God shone this infinite light into a space He created for the world to exist. But this light was far too spiritually intense for a physical world to contain. He therefore performed a process call Tzimtzum (covering) whereby He first passed His infinite light through a series of filters to lower its intensity to a level that this world would be able to withstand. This process is mirrored in the physical world when looking at a very high-intensity light. It is too bright to bear and can be injurious without wearing sunglasses or other forms of filters to decrease the intensity of the light. By dimming the light, we actually see more of it. Similarly, if you were to try to plug your radio into the main power plant of your city, it would just explode from too much power. We therefore need a series of resistors to bring the power down to the voltage of your radio. Similarly, as God shines his light down into our world, he uses a series of ten filters referred to as *sefirot*. This prepares the world to be ready for man to experience within the lower level that we were created. These filters reduce the light to a level that makes it possible for us to exist in the world.

A central theme in Kabbalah is that everything in the physical world is a reflection of something in the spiritual world, so to better understand sefirot, let's look at a prism. The light shining into the prism is just a clear white light with no identifiable colors. Once the light goes through the prism, seven colors appear on the other side. These colors were not created by the prism; rather, they were already embedded in the white light before hitting the prism, but we just couldn't identify them until they were refracted by the prism.

Similarly, as God shines His Endless Light into this world, it passes through a series of ten filters, each one containing and emitting one of His Divine attributes in the form of the ten sefirot. The seven lower sefirot relate directly to the world we live in, much like the seven colors shining through the prism. We will soon see how each of these attributes influences the world as a whole and defines the anatomy of our souls.

HOW CAN I BE "CREATED IN THE IMAGE OF GOD" IF GOD IS NOT PHYSICAL?

It seems almost like idol worship to describe man as being created in the image of God. After all, it is forbidden to make an image of God. That is a form of idolatry since it implies that God has physical properties. Yet the same Torah seems to express the opposite by saying that we as humans are created in God's image. To answer this question, we must first understand that the expression of the ten sefirot was not just applied to the world as a whole. The soul of man is also created using the same ten sefirot, and therefore we too are created as a reflection of God's attributes. As it says, "In the image of God He created Him".[1] Since God is infinite, the sefirot cannot be a physical image of God Himself. Rather, they are the Divine attributes with which He creates and expresses himself in this world and above. They are not a description of God Himself, only those qualities or attributes which He uses in relating to our world. Man was also, on some level, created as an expression of the same attributes. This is one of the explanations of what it means to be created in the image of God. . . created with the same Godly attributes with which He expresses Himself in relationship to this world.

There is much to learn about the significance of the location of each of the sefirot within the human body. To begin, let's look at the big picture, where we find the top three sefirot associated with the mind. There we find the intellectual attributes, *Chachma, Bina* and *Daat* (wisdom, understanding and knowledge). The lower seven sefirot are considered emotional attributes, and they are called *Chesed,*

---

1 Genesis 1:27

Gevurah, Tiferet, Netzach, Hod, Yesod and *Malchut* (kindness, restraint, harmony, victory, appreciation, foundation and kingship).

Many kabbalistic writings include a *sefira* above the mind called *Keter,* which means crown. Just as a crown sits above the head, not part of the actual body, so does the sefira of Keter. Keter is much like the point where light initially hits a prism in that it is the first point of contact where the endless light lands above our Divine soul before being split, first into the intellectual attributes and then down into the lower seven (like the seven colors seen through a prism). Let's take a look at the rainbow of sefirot that makes every one of us a Divine soul created in the "image of God."

This picture shows the placement of each of the sefirot on the human body and how they relate to the position of the sefirot in the creation of the world.

The Divine attributes in THE CREATION OF MAN

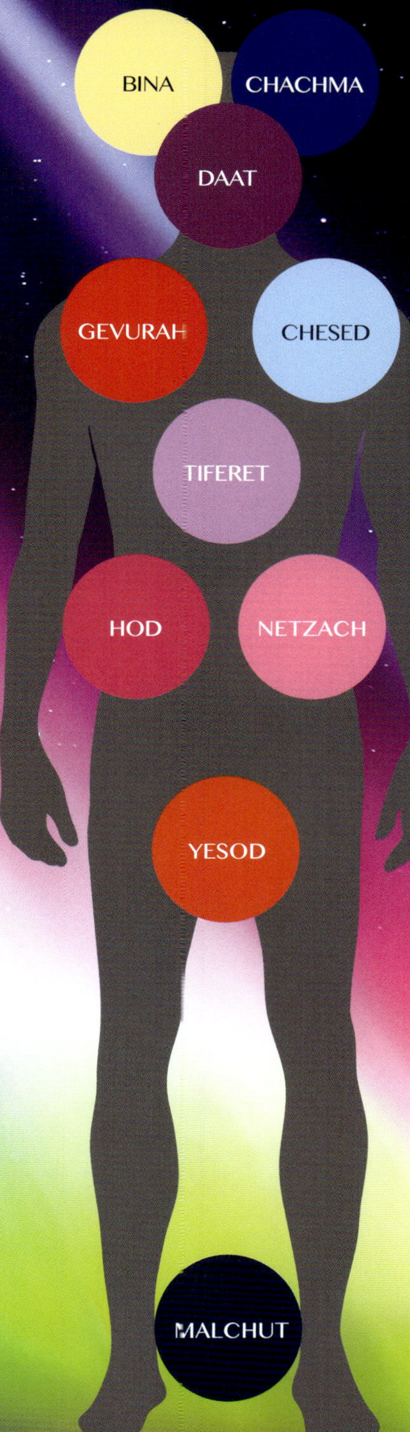

NESHAMA
BINA
CHACHMA
DAAT
GEVURAH
CHESED
TIFERET
HOD
NETZACH
YESOD
MALCHUT
RUACH
BINA
CHACHMA
DAAT
GEVURAH
CHESED
TIFERET
HOD
NETZACH
YESOD
MALCHUT
NEFESH
BINA
CHACHMA
DAAT
GEVURAH
CHESED
TIFERET
HOD
NETZACH
YESOD
MALCHUT

DNA OF THE SOUL

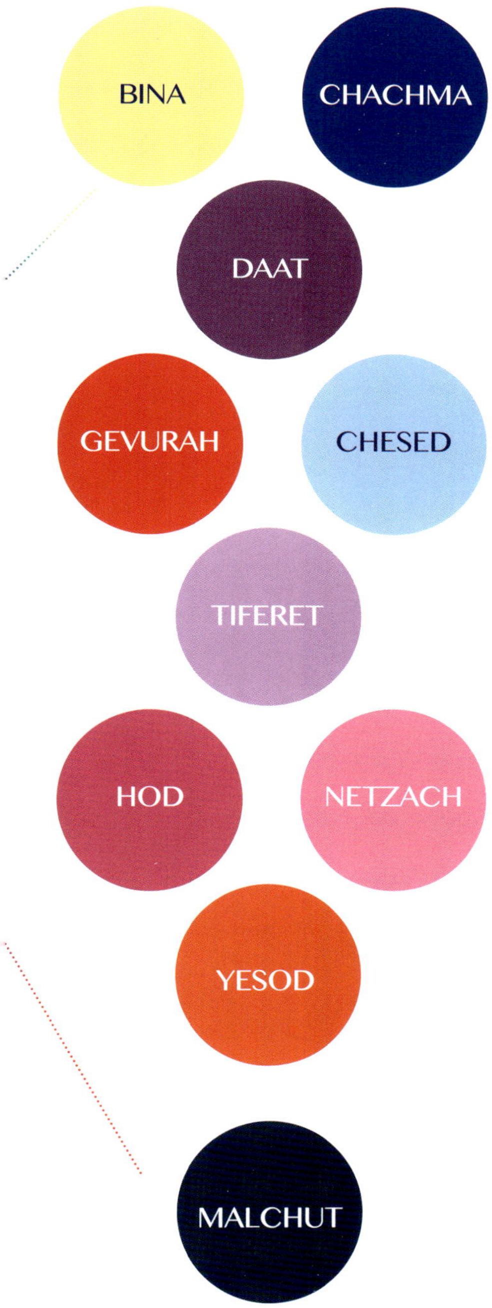

Another way we see how the physical world is a reflection of the spiritual is by looking at the anatomy of the soul. Besides the overall placement of each sefira within the soul, each level also contains a subgroup of ten sefirot. In a way, the ten sefirot are like the spiritual DNA of the soul. In this picture, you can see the ten sefirot within the Chesed of Ruach. The same structure is embedded in all the sefirot. It is fascinating to realize that scientists have only recently discovered that DNA is composed of patterns of letters that encode the whole body. Trillions of cells each contain within them the complete design of that individual person. This is a reflection of the same process that God used in creating the world and, more specifically, man. In Genesis, God created the world using ten statements. His speech, composed of sequences of letters, went beyond the level of thought and created attributes outside Himself using spoken words to bring them into existence. The ten statements are each associated with one of the ten sefirot, and just as in the physical realm letters are the building blocks of creation, so too we find the parallel structure in the anatomy of the soul. Within every one of the ten sefirot is a smaller cellular structure of the ten sefirot ultimately created through God's speaking out letters.

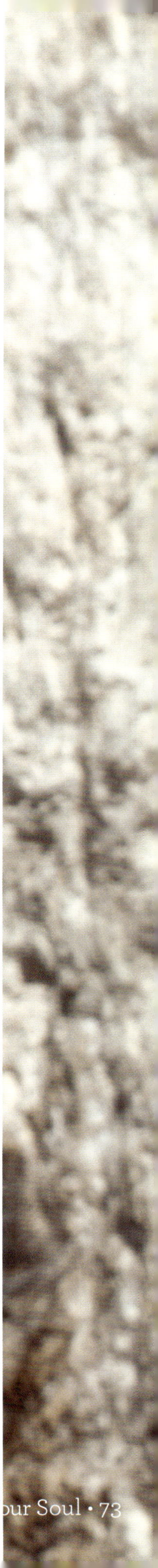

The Divine soul is always motivated to express its pure objectives, utilizing the ten Godly attributes. If it didn't have to battle against the animal soul, it would be a perfect personification of Godliness, much like Adam and Eve before the original sin. As we will discuss, each of the sefirot fulfills a profound function in addition to its relationship to the other attributes. Before we delve deeper into how the sefirot bring God's light from the highest point all the way down to the most tangible lowest level of Malchut, it is important to first see the big picture of how the ten sefirot are manifested within the animal soul, as well.

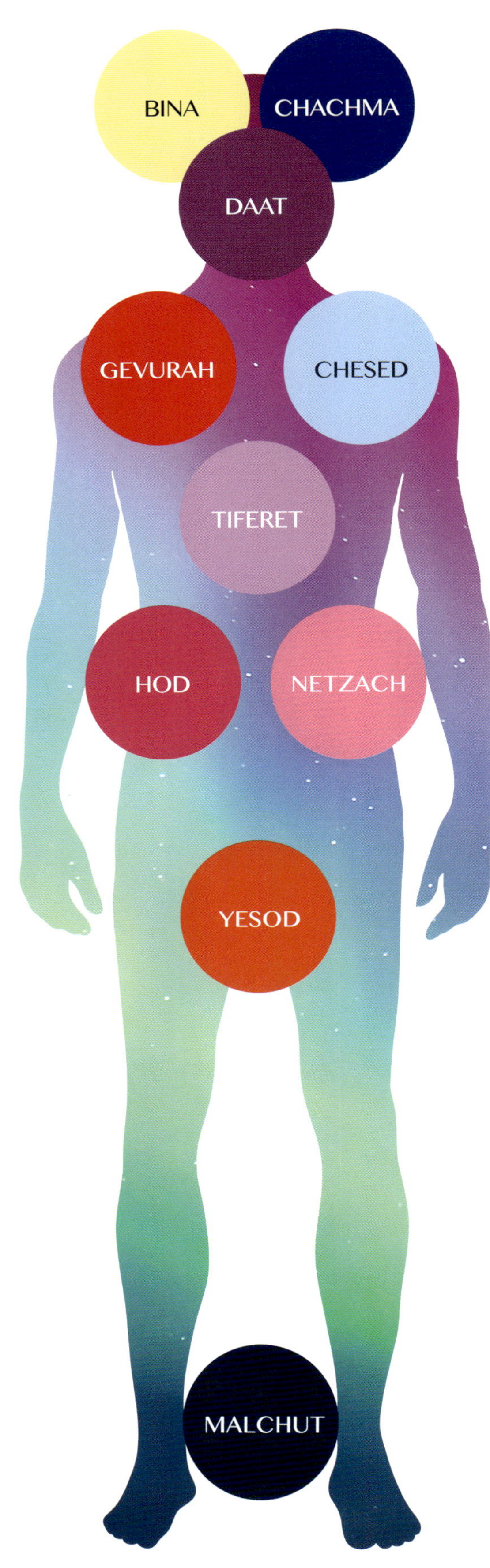

IS MY ANIMAL SOUL ALSO CREATED WITH THE TEN SEFIROT?

When we look deeper into the anatomy of the animal soul, we find the ten sefirot expressed in a negative, impure way. Each of the attributes is expressed using their potentially positive attributes but instead for self-indulgent reasons. The negative expressions of the ten sefirot within the animal soul are disguised in a way that appears to be like the positive attributes of the Divine soul. But they are not being channeled into holiness. Rather, they worship the ego rather than God, resulting in no moral obligations and dignity. For example, misguided chesed (kindness) can be used for very misleading and immoral purposes (e.g., taking advantage of others while appearing to be generous and caring). Most people have experienced being manipulated by people in this deceptive manner. Similarly, someone can utilize the attribute of Gevurah, which in the Divine soul, expresses important boundaries, discipline and self-control. But when Gevurah is conveyed by the animal soul, it is expressed by the egocentric need for power, control and oppression. This twisted, spiritual distortion is far too often used as a way to persuade people to follow religious cults. They use that which appears to be holy to lure people to believe lies while making them think that what they are exploring is pure holiness. This is a form of idol worship, using holiness as a powerful lie to get people to worship that which is profane.

Each of the ten sefirot within the animal soul has its way of misleading us through the twisted and negative expression of its attribute. We need to strengthen our insight and ability to detect whether the Divine attributes are being expressed purely or if they are motivated by the animal soul.

HOW DO MY THOUGHTS AFFECT MY DIVINE SOUL?

The Divine soul is compared to water—cool, composed and rational. Its behavior is the reverse of the animal soul in that it already has a crystal-clear awareness of the greatness of God. When we focus our mind in deep contemplation on holy thoughts and develop a greater understanding of Godliness, the energy of the Divine soul inspires the cold, intellectual tempered love to flow from the mind down to the right ventricle of the heart where there is no blood. There, it is expressed as a powerful emotional awareness of God, as it says in Kohelet,[1] "Lev chacham yemini," a wise heart on my right. For those who can reach such a lofty level, their spiritual awareness can then spread through the body, elevating it to the point where even the Klipat Noga of the animal soul is elevated to serve God. We will soon see additional pictures illustrating what we can do to invigorate the whole body to be uplifted by the positive energy emanating from the Divine soul. This is a very challenging level to achieve. The animal soul will fight you every step of the way, but again, it is important to remember that the animal soul is sent by the king to create a challenge for the prince, so it is one that we are all capable of overcoming. The battle is necessary to allow your Divine soul to keep you inspired with a strong intellectual and emotional awareness of God. This closeness to God is what our souls are sent into this world to strive toward. Now let's build our ammunition by taking a closer look at the inner workings of the battle between your two souls.

---

1 Kohelet 12

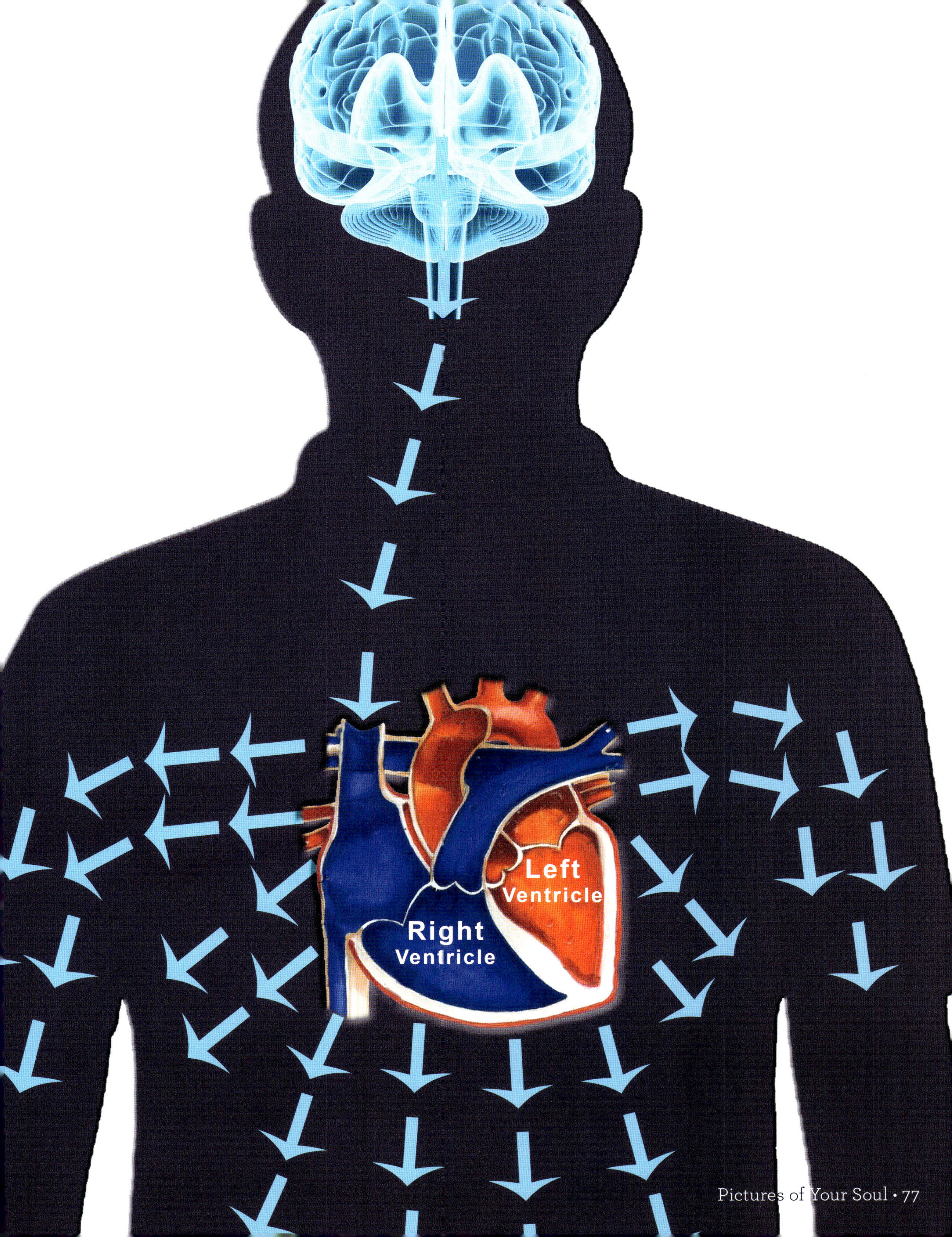
Left
Ventricle
Right
Ventricle

ZOOMING IN

WHY DO I FEEL LIKE I AM IN THE MIDST OF A RAGING INTERNAL BATTLE?

As we have discussed, we live with a constant inner battle between the Divine soul and the animal soul, both trying to gain control of all parts of the body. The *Tanya* compares the body to a small city fought over by two kings, each one trying to gain control of as much territory as possible. The conquest of every neighborhood is a significant victory since its citizens will then serve whichever king has established control. Both souls want to take control of the body because that is their only tangible way to express themselves in this physical world. Without the use of the body, the soul would be unarmed without the means to achieve its purpose in this life. But both souls are given a fair chance at winning over the body and its useful qualities and attributes. This is why we must struggle to win the battle so our Divine soul can serve as the king that rules over as much of the "city" as possible.

Ultimately, both souls want to win you over to implement their agenda. This becomes a challenge, for it is your free-will choice to identify yourself as a dignified person with a high level of spiritual awareness and a strong determination to do that which is moral and productive. Or, conversely, if you identify yourself with your animal soul, your self-

image will depend upon living your life to fulfill the "pleasures" of the animal soul, and you will continue to be dominated by its rule. For example, someone who has an addiction to gambling knows it is self-destructive, but after continuing to succumb, they no longer fight to win over the addiction. They view gambling as intrinsic to their identity. The animal soul is trying to subvert all your attributes by diminishing you to a low enough point where you see yourself as a person who just behaves according to the animal soul and from day to day sees no reason to change. By persisting in this self-destructive behavior, as victims of the dominance of their animal soul, they become more and more unconscious of their Divine soul and unable to enjoy what a meaningful life can offer them.

You can rightly ask why would a loving God put us in such a ruthless battle, especially since the animal soul, assisted by advertising, movies, the internet and popular culture extolling bodily pleasures, has so much ammunition, making it seemingly impossible for the Divine soul to win the battle and live a spiritual life. As mentioned earlier, this battle is really a gift that enables us to exercise our free will. This is one of the primary attributes that differentiates us from animals. If we had not been created with an animal soul, we would not be challenged to do anything that is not good and would therefore lack the ability to achieve anything of our own. In truth, in this confusing and very enticing world, the animal soul is given more strength to win over the Divine soul, but if we do our best in the battle to live a meaningful life, we can prevail. God steps in and lovingly lifts us above our natural inclinations, giving us the ability to achieve much more than we would otherwise achieve on our own. So, as we discuss some techniques to win over the animal soul, don't be discouraged if it seems very daunting. We must always focus on the next step in our personal growth, or we are likely to stumble.

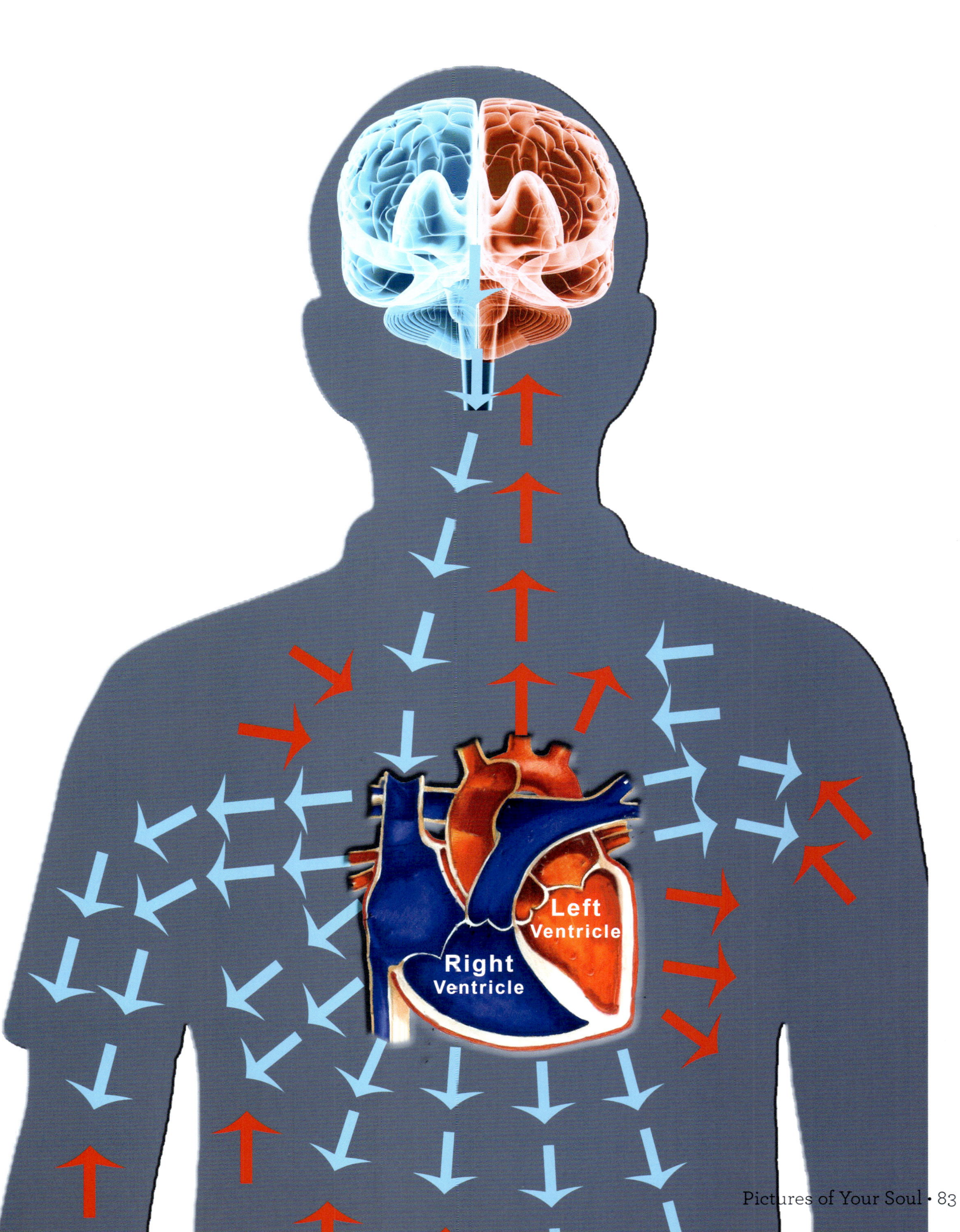
Left
Ventricle
Right
Ventricle

CLARITY VS. CONFUSION

From the above, you have seen how the animal soul is the king of deception. One of its primary techniques involves confusing your mind, making you think that what you really want can only be achieved by submitting to the animal soul's command. Creating confusion is one of the primary tactics of the animal soul's battle plan because once you have entertained the lies, you are extremely vulnerable, and you have already lost half the battle. A temptation that you once knew to be wrong gradually becomes twisted into being a realistic consideration. Then your desires work to push you further and further until you become sufficiently rationalized and then convinced so you don't see anything wrong and/or you don't believe you have the self-control to engage in a battle. The animal soul has won a major victory, so any subsequent effort to overcome the animal soul becomes even harder. Rav Noach Weinberg z'l used to always say "clarity or death." "Know what you know and know what you don't know." We must be honest with what we are confused about, for that is where we are most vulnerable. Again, being humble about our capabilities is essential to our success.

TAKING CONTROL

It is a given that one must be particularly strong in acquiring and holding onto a firm awareness of what is truly the wish of our Divine soul, which is the real you vs. what may superficially seem just as spiritually or physically enticing but is really the work of the animal soul creating more confusion. This is exactly what the snake did in the Garden of Eden to get Eve to eat from the forbidden tree. He created deceptive arguments to confuse her into thinking she would actually be fulfilling God's intention by eating from the tree. After Adam and Eve ate, one of the main punishments was confusion. No longer was right and wrong, good and bad a clear choice. The animal soul, containing Klipat Noga, a mixture of good and bad, then became the norm, and the voice of the snake became an internal voice constantly working to create the confusion used to seduce us into making the bad choices.

A meaningful life demands fighting for clarity, for without it, we are victims of confusion. Clarity is not something that one acquires and then owns; for even the best of us, it is a constant challenge and struggle to maintain it. The more one learns about the soul and how it works, the more one can acquire the tools to hold on tight and use the ammunition required to win the inner battle.

In the Torah, we learn about Yosef, who faced an extremely difficult challenge. Yosef was living in the house of Potifar, whose wife tried to seduce him day after day until she became seemingly irresistible. The sages teach us that Yosef's lustful desire had become unimaginably challenging. He had come so close to being seduced that he already envisioned falling to his desires. His animal soul was clearly winning the inner battle. But when Yosef saw a reflection of himself, his resemblance to his father served as a flash of clarity as to who he was, where he came from and the standard of morality that he was obligated to maintain. This was a powerful breakthrough of clarity that enabled him to suddenly find the strength to escape the overwhelming temptation, even while Potifar's wife threatened to have Yosef thrown in jail as if he was the one trying to seduce her. The more we can attach ourselves to what we know is true and noble, the more clarity we can acquire, the more armed we will be in the battle against the confusion created by the animal soul.

SPIRITUAL PLEASURES ARE ETERNAL

One important step in our efforts to acquire the type of clarity that saved Yosef involves learning how to differentiate between the voice of the animal soul and that of the truth. You should be familiar with the voice of the animal soul when it is trying to convince you to fulfill a temporary pleasure. An animalistic experience ends as soon as it is over. Even though it was sold to you as the greatest lasting pleasure that you can't forgo, the truth is that once you have indulged, the experience is gone. Once you have enjoyed the experience, the animal soul needs to look for new ways to either sell you on indulging in more of the same pleasure or moving on to the next superficial high.

This eternal pleasure of the Divine soul is the opposite of the temporary pleasure of the animal soul.

The opposite is true about the pleasures of the Divine soul, which are eternal. They continue within you for your lifetime and even after you leave this world. They testify on your behalf before the heavenly tribunal. As a concrete example, imagine yourself in a situation where you saw someone hovering between life and death, and you were the only one to stop what you were doing and run to help him, becoming the hero who actually saved his life. He thanked you profusely, and then you went on with your own life. The admirable event was over... but not really, because even years later, you can think about your heroic act and still feel a sense of fulfillment from having done something so incredibly meaningful. Thus, you have achieved an eternal pleasure, which will always be to your credit in that account in which your positive thoughts and actions are inscribed. This account can serve as your ammunition against the animal soul because this eternal pleasure of the Divine soul is the opposite of the temporary pleasure of the animal soul. Each truly uplifting experience can serve as a powerful lesson and reminder on how to evaluate enticing and seductive choices. Will you still feel the pleasure after the action has been experienced, or will it quickly fade?

This does not mean that God wants to discourage you from enjoying physical pleasures. He loves you and is not looking to deprive you of healthy pleasure and self-expression. He made a world full of delights, and we are encouraged to enjoy them. In fact, so many of the Torah's commandments are connected to physical pleasures. For example, on Shabbat we are supposed to eat three meals. People save their money to buy the finest and most appealing food to ensure that their shabbat meals are as tasty and filling as possible. Although the body enjoys these delights, they are still spiritually enjoyable since they are connected to the commandment of keeping and honoring Shabbat. With this consciousness in mind, we must eat with dignity rather than indulge purely in the physical aspect of the pleasure. We must enjoy the physical pleasure as Divine souls created in the image of God.

With regard to the animal soul, we shouldn't wait for an all-out war to work on building our combat skills. An expert in Karate doesn't wait to be facing his enemy in a dark alley before figuring out a winning strategy. Self-defense training involves ongoing drills and exercises to be prepared for any scenario. They practice defensive and offensive moves, which are reflexively triggered by any threatening move by their opponent. With enough practice, self-defense becomes second nature without having to think very much about how to respond, becoming programmed into your subconscious mind. Similarly, by learning all we can about the nature of the Divine soul and animal soul and about our individual vulnerabilities, you can train yourself to be like the Karate expert ready for any battle that comes your way.

FROM DARKNESS TO LIGHT

So many people live their lives without any consideration of what they truly are longing to express. They are trapped into believing that Hollywood represents the ultimate success and desired way of life. Their role models are the rich and famous; people model their lives on those who, behind the camera, are proportionally more prone to drug abuse, depression and even suicide. Their inner city has been conquered, and the Divine soul has been kept out of the battle. By having such powerful role models, people's life goals represent the meaningless expression of selfish indulgence. Emulating these icons of popular culture increases their susceptibility to dangerous, life-threatening addictions as they pursue the "pleasures" of the animal soul.

So many people have fallen to such point of desperation that they are unable to pull themselves up without the help of someone else who can help them open their minds and hearts to see that life can be so much more meaningful and truly pleasurable. They need to be shown the genuine, enduring opportunities that are available to them should they break their negative behavioral habits. The lower they have sunk into these habits, the harder it is to change their mindset and value system immersed in superficial desires. Sadly, victims of such spiritual and emotional suffering see no reason to change. Oblivious to a higher level of life, they appear to be having the time of their lives, indulging in any pleasure coming their way.

Having given the power over to the animal soul, they do not have the discipline, responsibility and self-control to avoid every momentary indulgence. Unfortunately, their animal soul has become so powerful that the Divine soul is quiet by comparison and lacking in ammunition. How can you help someone who is so deeply immersed in such emptiness? They think you are absolutely crazy for suggesting any other way of life. How can you reach them when their own addictions and self-destructive behaviors have enabled them to be completely captured by the animal soul. Why should they listen to a word you have to say?

A SMALL STEP FORWARD

An effective way to help his/her ascent is to find whatever meaningful experience they still can recognize and bring it to their attention as a starting point. For example, getting them to help someone else can provide a motivational place to build from. An altruistic effort can develop their awareness of the pleasure of the Divine soul. The more they appreciate the quality of such a pleasure, the more receptive they will be to advice about conducting their life with more dignified behavior. This can be a slow process, but if they see that you are sincere in wanting to help them, you can open the door to saving someone's life.

Among the programs I have taught for is a center here in Israel for drug rehabilitation. I felt the urge to yank the student out of his negative, self-destructive mindset and provide him with a taste of spiritual awakening to get him on the road to recovery. Of course, that was what the staff were doing in a methodical therapeutic way. I have seen many people who are so addicted to destructive thinking about themselves, they are scared to see themselves in a positive light. They have no concept of being created in the image of God with a Divine soul at the root of who they really are.

In some cases, even with help, people sink to such a low level that there is nowhere to go but up. It's only from that very low dark pit that if they look up, they will get a glimpse of the potential for good. "How did I get here?" they ask themselves. "This is not the real me. I deserve a more dignified life rather than living in the gutter, void of meaning and true happiness." I'm not just describing someone who is homeless or suffering from substance abuse. This type of awakening also applies to people who are viewed as successful yet are suffering from being workaholics or indulgence in ongoing immoral behavior. They ask themselves, "Why am I a slave to my work and financial success?" "Why can't I stop to enjoy my family and friends?" "Why have I become addicted to watching inappropriate videos on the internet?" "Everything is about money, image and other forms of self-indulgence." "I wish I could just live my life filled with what really matters and not care about my image."

When they finally get a glimpse of clarity, and they are able to sustain this awareness, this glimpse can initiate the spark of determination, the *chachma* (wisdom) to begin their journey back to a spiritually healthy life. Often this ascent provides them with the will, discipline and coping skills to reach an even higher spiritual level than where they were before, falling prey to the animal soul. Many books have been written by people who lifted themselves up from such a low level to an even higher place of personal redemption. Once they taste the beauty and meaning of spiritual growth, they find the inner drive to continue growing.

It is important to keep in mind that apathy is also a tool of the animal soul, and the inner battle rages on even if you decide not to care. Its voice is louder and will win the battle unless you consciously put up a strong fight to protect yourself. But once again, you should keep in mind that God helps those who put in the effort to be helped. You will be surprised by what you can achieve once you begin your ascent. The following song was written to reach such people whose negative thinking dominates their lives.

BACK TO YOUR SOUL

(realyouproject.com/music)

Between your mind lines
Giving up on mankind
Like you're running out of time
Slowly falling

Living half dead
Barely holding by a thread
Try to catch your own breath
Hear your calling

(Chorus)
'Cause it's time
To open your eyes
And reach for the skies above you
Pray to survive
And shine you with heavenly love
Where you know he will take you
Where nothing can break you
And bring you back in touch with your soul

Trying to survive the lies
But it's eating you up alive
And you're holding it all inside
Barely crying

Too many false starts
And it's breaking your world apart
So just hold on to your heart
Hear your calling

Chorus

WWW.REALYOUPROJECT.COM/B

SCAN TO LISTEN

HELP! HOW DO I COME OUT VICTORIOUS?

THE PATH OF CONTEMPLATION

Regardless of your spiritual level, there are techniques that you can use to achieve tremendous heights, even from a low starting point. Although our goal is to develop a strong love and awe of God, this does not mean that we must be on fire in our passion for every commandment or act of kindness we do. Rather, there is a level of love and awe that is more measured yet still expressed from the heart. The *Tanya* discusses two main paths to achieving this love of God. The first is the path of contemplation, where we use our intellectual attributes to develop our connection. Rather than performing a commandment strictly because it is the right thing to do, one can first contemplate God's love for us. Think about the awesomeness of His creation and the gift of the profound relationships in our lives. This will generate a type of love that still resides primarily in the mind but can serve as an inspiration to perform the commandments with more feeling and enthusiasm.

Two Paths of Personal Growth

Before addressing any specific commandment, we must trust that if we invest our time and effort to use

our minds to contemplate the greatness and awesomeness of God and His creation; we will be inspired to experience feelings of love and awe. On the macrocosmic level, contemplate the brilliant design of our world and the solar system. Then on a microcosmic level, think of the trillions of cells and DNA encoded in our bodies. How can this complexity and perfection be merely a fluke of nature or a consequence of evolution? Our human capacity for ingenuity, creativity and profound philosophical thought, our sense of justice and compassion, our deep and nuanced relationships with family and friends indicate an intelligent design is obvious.

Our contemplation on the amazing design of the universe and every part of it inspires us to love and revere our creator.

Our contemplation on the amazing design of the universe and every part of it inspires us to love and revere our creator. Moving forward from these feelings can motivate us to integrate spirituality into our daily lives.

Once you have worked hard to gain this awareness, the challenge is to hold on to it, especially since the animal soul will continue its battle to reconquer your mind and heart with confusion and tempting desires to pull you away. This is the lifelong battle that even those whom we think of as being spiritually accomplished or righteous must face on a daily level. Continued meditation as well as prayer and Torah learning can help you maintain your ascent. Your success in this most important endeavor of your life will make you more and more aware of your place in the realm of spirituality where God's miracles abound. Through this path of contemplation, you are accumulating the tools that allow your Divine soul to be expressed.

THE PATH OF WAKING UP THE HIDDEN LOVE

The second approach to waking up your love and awe of God is based on the understanding that we have been created with inner love and awe already within us. It is incredible that this innate love of God is heartfelt by so many people of all spiritual levels, even those who seem to be totally removed from this understanding. It is a historical fact that in times of persecution, many people who were not observant at all were still willing to die rather than worship an idol. It makes no sense given the fact that they lived a totally secular life, never indicating any interest in religious practice or a connection with God. Many of them claimed to be atheists and even anti-religious, yet they were willing to sacrifice their lives rather than commit such a severe violation. This love of God resides in all of us; this inner faith is like a sixth sense asserting itself when threatened. Even if it seems dormant, we all have a deep longing to experience a connection with our creator.

This inner faith is like a sixth sense asserting itself when threatened.

The *Tanya* explains that this intuitive love is part of our spiritual inheritance from our forefathers who lived with love and awe of God on a level much beyond our comprehension, and they implanted this love into our spiritual DNA. Rather than waiting for our lives to be threatened or to submit to the power of the animal soul, we have the ability to uncover this hidden love, allowing it to surface, knowing that it is an integral part of who we are. Therefore, we are now about to explore how to bring this love into our daily lives.

An important equation to be aware of is that since you would be willing to give your life, which is the ultimate sacrifice, to prevent severing your connection with God, then you certainly have the inner will to make less consequential sacrifices. Therefore, when the opportunity arises to do what is seemingly a small *mitzvah*,

you have a hidden reservoir of love of God within you to channel into its fulfillment. If you are willing to give up everything for your connection to God, why not seize the opportunity to perform many deeds to achieve the same goal without having to give up your life. So the first step in uncovering your love of God is remembering the inner will that is already part of you. As the *Tanya* quotes, "For this thing is very near to you, in your mouth and in your heart, that you may do it,"[1] meaning that the nature of this inner love is always within reach of your subconscious mind and heart, and we must do our best to make it an actual experience. And like a candle whose flame is always reaching upward, longing for a connection to its source, so too our soul is reaching up in its longing for a loving connection with our Creator. It just takes a little digging to uncover.

The first step in uncovering your love of God is remembering the inner will that is already part of you.

Especially for today's generation, we face a growing challenge to our awareness of this hidden love. We are increasingly distracted by all the noise that confuses our minds and hearts. If we were able to quiet the voices of the animal soul advocating for all the enticements that surround us, it would be so much easier to become aware of our inner love. Unfortunately, we are just too distracted by all the ongoing buzz from phones, work, recreational activities and social life. These all have their positive uses, but as soon as they take over our lives, the intrinsic inner love gets pushed down below our consciousness.

We must therefore dig for gold where we know

---

1 deuteronomy 30:11

there truly is a goldmine. It should not be a hopeless search for inner happiness; the inner flame is burning inside us, but until we lower the noise inundating us from all directions, we won't feel what we are already intuitively longing for. So dig down, quiet the noise, breathe deeply, focus on your inner self and get in touch with the burning flame that is within you, longing to be realized.

To help you gain a more mindful awareness of your "inner love," take a listen to the title song from my album *Empty Spaces*. Here are the lyrics.

EMPTY SPACES

Breathe into the moment
Eyes closed to the world outside
Tune in to the silence
Let go and slowly lift my mind

Through the empty
Empty spaces
Let me feel the wonders of my soul

What am I feeling? What am I thinking?
Let it all just drift on by
Inner healing, feel the freedom
Just surrender and let me slowly rise

Through empty
Empty spaces
Let me feel the wonders of my soul

WWW.REALYOUPROJECT.COM/E

SCAN TO LISTEN

WHEN AM I CONSIDERED SUCCESSFUL?

We must be careful not to buy into the notion that true success is only achieved when we have completely defeated the enemy within. That is not the Jewish concept of success. In fact, if you theoretically were able to completely eradicate the animal soul, you would negate your free will and have nothing to strive for and achieve through your own efforts. Rather, someone who humbly struggles with ruling over his or her animal soul is already successful. Facing up to the challenge of conquering our physical desires is a hugely noble endeavor even if we don't always "succeed." Giving yourself credit for this effort will have a profound effect on your ability to conquer additional challenges. The more you make this awareness a critical part of your thinking, the easier it will be to act from within that positive mindset of success.

Someone who humbly struggles with ruling over his or her animal soul is already successful.

BUT WHAT IF I FAIL AND FALL TO SIN?

Welcome to the human race. Although repentance involves a process that cleanses ourselves of sin, we must be aware of the distance between us and God that is widened when we sin. The more we have developed our love and awe of God, the more painfully we feel this distance, and that helps prevent ourselves from falling. Meanwhile, once we have sinned, it is critical to take the positive steps to use the gift of repentance to undo the damage and diminish the distance we have created. In a way, repentance does not make sense. How can one undo the spiritual damage caused by sinning? By following a method set out by the Torah, forgiveness is granted, and then we are ready to do our best to return at least to the level we were at before. Think positively and trust you have been forgiven and can move forward.

Think positively and trust you have been forgiven and can move forward.

One of the dangerous techniques of the animal soul is to beat you up after you have fallen. This makes you label yourself as a failure and paralyzes your ability to continue on your spiritual path. It is critical to know that after you have fallen, you must recognize that it is the voice of the animal soul in full force that is screaming that you are a failure, that you are guilty and not worthy of reaching higher heights. The voice knocking you down is not a holy voice demanding a higher level of spirituality. Learn to get up and continue to ascend on your holy mission, always remembering that the essence of who you are is created in the image of God, nothing less.

ARE ALL SOULS THE SAME?

No. Just as no two fingerprints are the same, no two souls are the same. Every soul is brought down into this world with its individual character and personality as well as its unique mission as to what it should achieve in its life. In my book entitled *A Book about You,* I discuss how we are all rooted in primary personalities and individual blends of Divine attributes. This understanding helps people go deeper on their individual path to discover what makes them unique and how to achieve that which God mandated them to do. Some souls are brought into this world on a higher spiritual level than others, but we must all work to grow from our individual level and unique challenges. The great Kabbalist Arizal said as follows: "Since the creation of the world, every day and every single moment is utterly unique, every person is utterly unique, and no one has the capacity to repair what his fellow repairs."

There is nothing more fulfilling than to be who you really are and live an active life that was meant for your unique soul. Everyone has to work together yet play his or her individual part in the symphony in order for the beauty of the composition to be expressed.

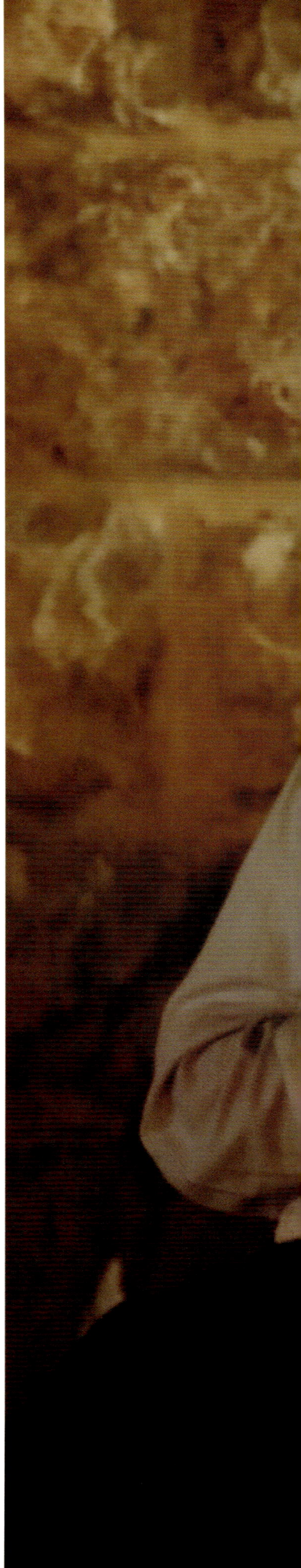

Every soul is brought down into this world with its individual character and personality.

SHEDDING LIGHT ON THE PICTURE

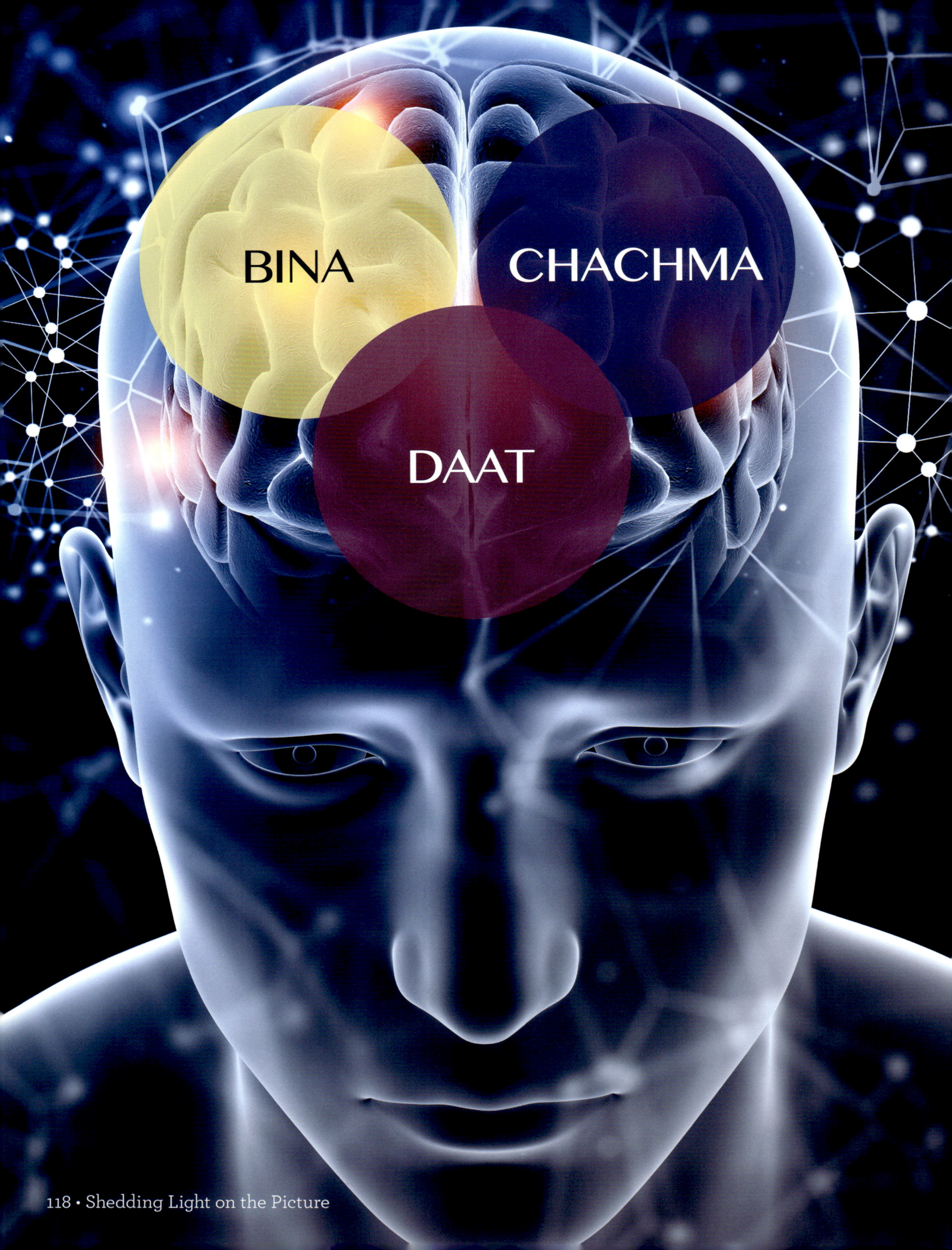
BINA
CHACHMA
DAAT

CAN UNDERSTANDING THE SOUL HELP ME BECOME MORE PRODUCTIVE IN MY DAY-TO-DAY LIFE?

Understanding the attributes of the soul teaches us a tremendous amount about how to be more productive in many areas of our lives. We can begin by taking a clearer picture of the intellectual attributes to see how they function within our thinking. This will not only help us in our internal battle, but by understanding how we function, we can learn how to use our minds more creatively and productively to gain greater self-control over our emotional well-being. So, although our primary focus is to develop our closeness to God, we will also see how the Divine attributes apply to our day to day thinking in a number of areas of life from business, creativity, relationships and to living a balanced life.

The three sefirot in the mind are referred to as the mothers of all the others since, like primary colors, they give birth to all those below. Let's explore the function and character of each one.

CHACHMA
WISDOM

Chachma, located in the right side of the brain, governs the initial spark of a seemingly insignificant idea that in fact really contains a vast amount of encoded information. It is a dot in its undeveloped seminal stage. Have you ever had a flash of an idea fly through your mind but had no idea what it really meant? We often make the mistake of underestimating the potential of a flicker of an idea, so we allow it to just drift away, without making the effort to capture the idea and unravel it to discover what it really means. That first spark is the attribute of Chachma providing you with a glimpse of an idea that you can choose to explore in more depth... or just let it escape your consciousness.

As we will see, Chachma is too abstract to exist on its own; it needs to proceed to the next level to become tangible enough to reveal the depth encoded inside the thought. It is important to become more aware of these seminal sparks of ideas that, if processed properly, can provide you with higher wisdom and direction in life. By becoming more mindful of the sparks being generated by your own Chachma, you can tap into a wealth of knowledge that can be life changing.

Chachma can also start with a more proactive approach. Rather than waiting for an idea to flash in your mind, you can learn to actively channel your thinking toward a general topic and allow your Chachma to start producing related abstract thoughts. A composer can brainstorm some undeveloped melodies and then grab a few inspirational notes that can become the foundation of a beautiful symphony.

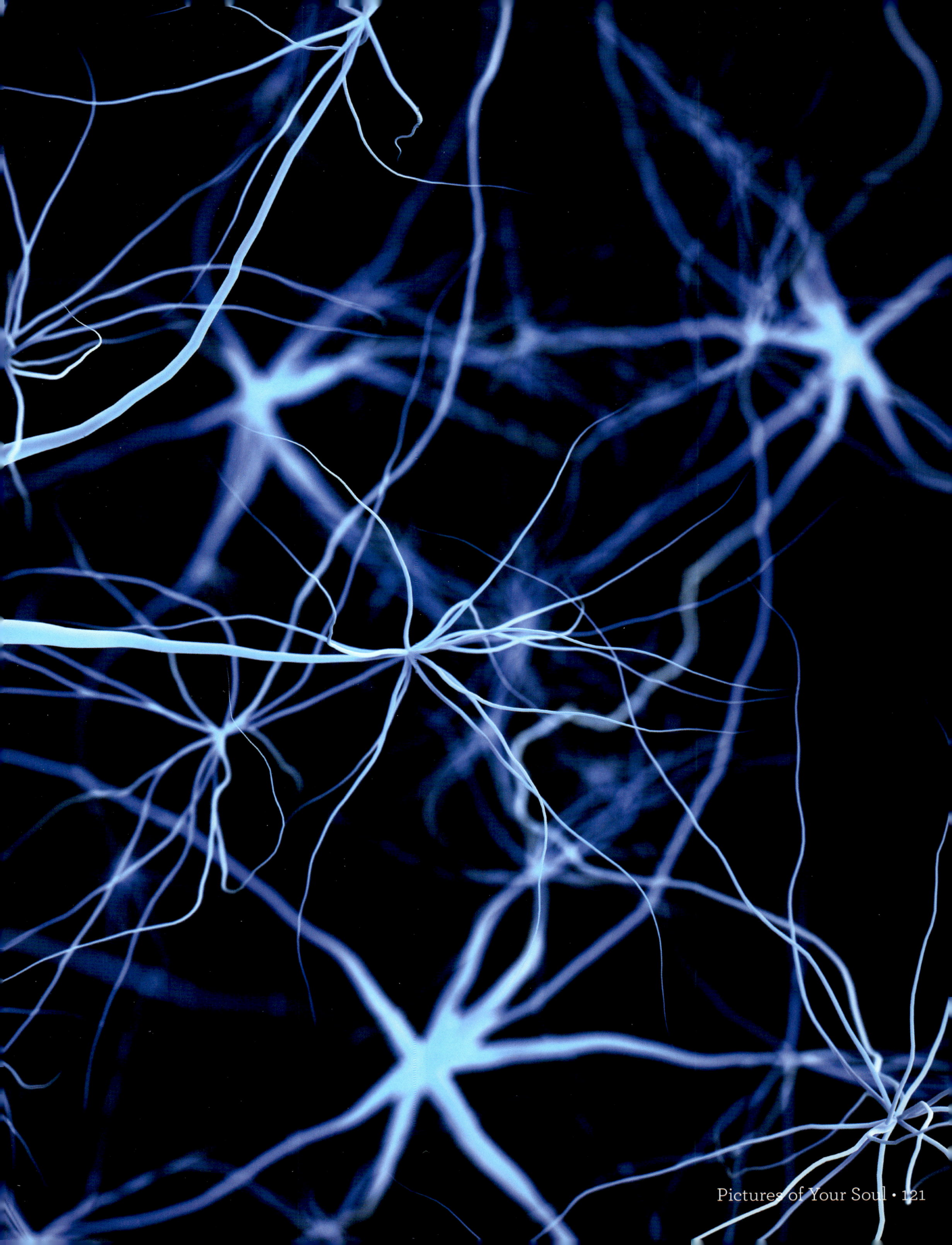

BINA
UNDERSTANDING

Bina, located in the left side of the brain, takes the spark from Chachma and begins to process it to a level of understanding and comprehension that is tangible to the cognitive mind. The idea is analyzed and sufficiently broken apart enough to become tangible to a point of great clarity and understanding. This takes effort, patience and determination, coupled with the optimism of knowing that the Chachma will provide you with the seed for a great opportunity for clarity. And with the proper Bina mindset, deep understanding will blossom. Not every flash of Chachma is worth pursuing. If you invest your Bina into it, you may decide that you have enough clarity to know that it is not a productive idea worth pursuing. In either case, it is worth trying to detect the potential of the idea. Once you have grabbed the abstract form of the idea, it's time to start to dissect it to see all of its components. Using your Bina is a natural skill, but it should also be a conscious process so that you can get the clarity required to take it to the next step.

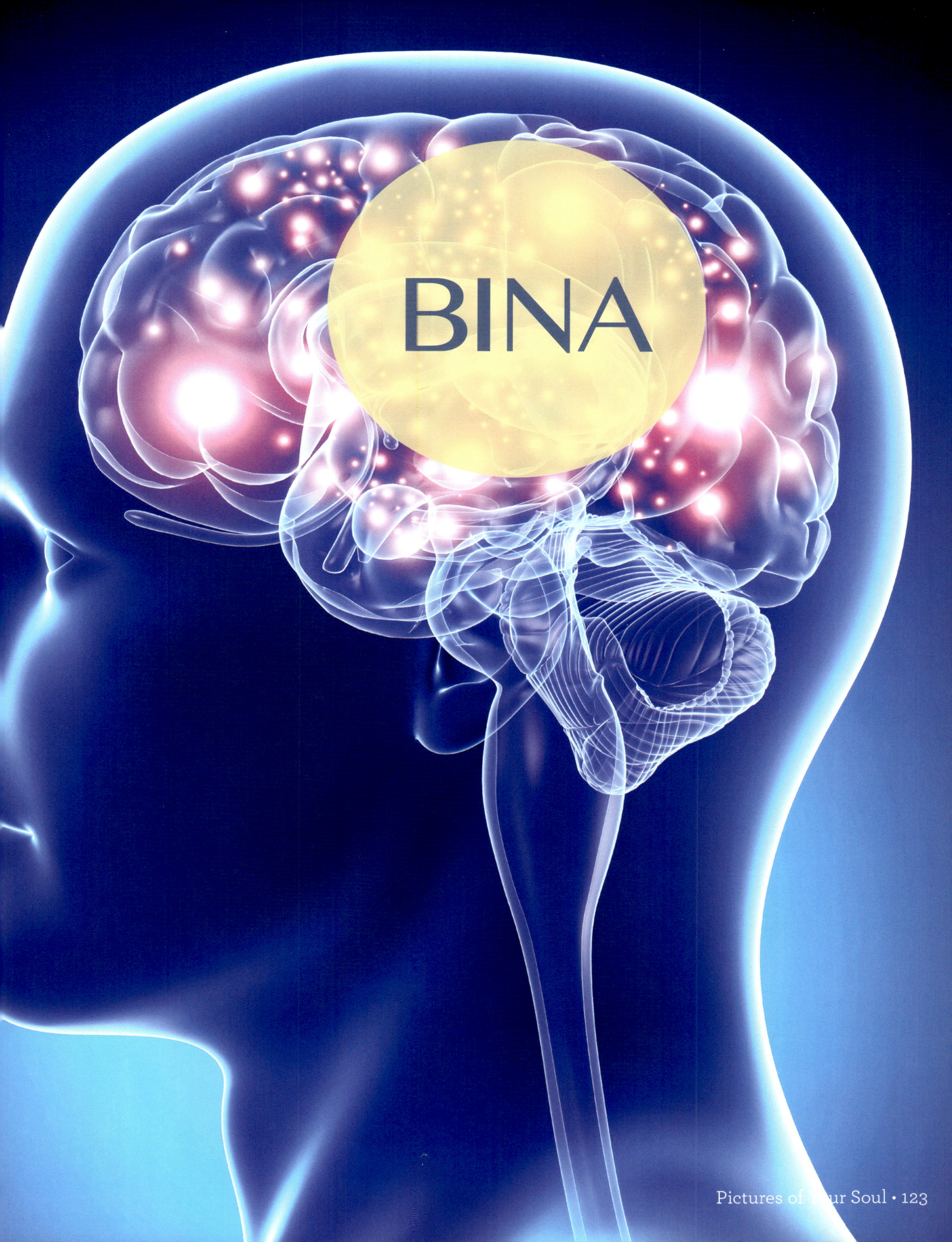
BINA

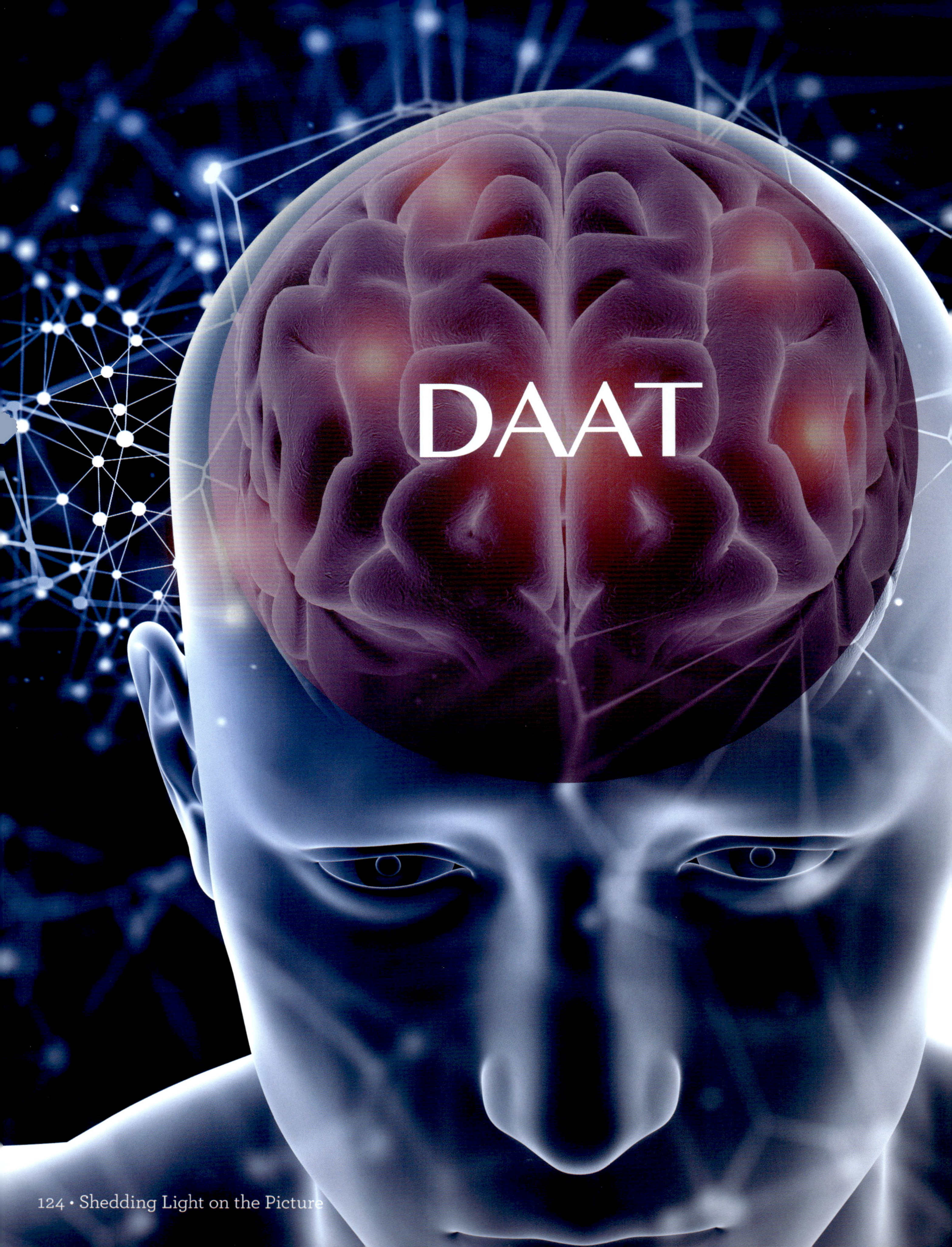
DAAT

DAAT
KNOWLEDGE

The union of wisdom and understanding (Chachma and Bina) are the father and mother who give birth to a much deeper integration of an idea into the sefira of Daat. This union is a very intimate connection between Chachma and Bina, which is compared to the union of Adam and Eve as it says, "Adam knew (Daat) Eve,"[1] denoting a deep, intimate connection. When you feel an idea crystalize to a point where it becomes a part of you, it has reached a stage of Daat. You now are living the idea, and the idea is very much alive. As mentioned earlier, Chachma, Bina and Daat are all important stages in the process of actualizing an idea. But it does not stop there, for God gave us these faculties to be used to elevate our souls through channeling them into our spiritual growth. Let's see how we can use these attributes for an even deeper awareness that will help us achieve the mission we are here to accomplish.

---

1 Gen 4:1

THE EMOTIONAL ATTRIBUTES

Once Daat has had a chance to be internalized, it gives birth to the emotional attributes, which are expressed through Chesed and Gevurah, the first two of the emotional Divine attributes. From there, they spread to all the other emotional attributes: Tiferet, Netach, Hod, Yesod and Malchut.

Let's briefly define these lower-emotional sefirot.

Chesed is the outpouring of pure altruistic love and endless giving. It expresses itself in the form of selfless productivity and creative energy and expression. It becomes a source of a continuous flow of generosity. Chesed has a similar nature to Chachma but within the emotional realm. It initiates an emotion expressed by total giving, and only later, it evolves into an expression that includes proper boundaries.

Gevurah creates barriers allowing Chesed to have the structure providing an essential framework for love to be expressed in a healthy way. The Divine attribute of Gevurah is what limits an overpowering presence of God in the world, thus allowing us to experience holiness within our limited capacity.

The remaining sefirot are less relevant to our discussion of the pictures of the soul. I will therefore provide a brief description of each:

TIFERET
BEAUTY & BALANCE

The trait of Tiferet is born out of the healthy balance of Chesed and Gevurah. It manifests itself in the amazing balance and harmony of creation. Inwardly, it creates the clarity to experience and act truthfully. Tiferet is not merely a combination of Chesed and Gevurah; it is a quality of its own that integrates both of them, much like Daat internalizes Chachma and Bina. Tiferet is located in the center of the body below Chesed and Gevurah.

NETZACH
DOMINANCE

Netzach, which means dominance or eternity, is a more physical representation of Chesed's expansive quality. (Thus, it sits under Chesed on the chart of the sefirot.) It represents the dynamic force that propels life and creation forward, the thrust of the universe outward from the center. It also represents God's eternal Word, which moves through history, influencing and elevating all of life. On the personal level, Netzach is expressed through leadership and imposing one's view on the world in a forceful way. It enables us to be clear about what we want to achieve and strives determinately to execute our intentions. Netzach is associated with the right thigh—the dominant leg that carries one forward in life.

HOD
SPLENDOR

Hod is located on the left thigh. It represents the passive admission and acceptance of whatever challenge we face. Rather than taking the offensive, Hod responds with empathy and employs strategies to keep the peace while allowing the challenge to pass as quietly as possible.

Yesod is the final channel through which God's light passes before entering this world. It manifests the perfect balance of expansion and contraction, as expressed in the preceding eight sefirot. It lies on the center column of the chart of the sefirot, and on the human level, it corresponds to the male reproductive organ, which is the channel through which the very essence of a man flows in the creation of new life. Yesod represents the perfect amount of satisfying the total need of the receiver without sacrificing the sanctity of the giver in any way. Similarly, Yesod represents the ability to become involved in the positive use of the physical world without being pulled down by negative influences. The stability of its internal spiritual strength is always strong enough to prevent such a falling.

Malchut is like a vessel that receives the light of all the upper sefirot and then humbly shares it with the world. Its function is to reveal the final combination of forces assembled above. Malchut represents kingship in that it brings all the higher levels down to earth and allows us to experience Godliness in the physical world. On the human frame, Malchut is associated with the mouth, which reveals the inner thoughts and feelings of the individual. It is also associated with the feet, which are the parts of the body that touch the earth. Malchut expresses total humility by allowing the content of the preceding sefirot to be expressed through it in the same way that King David was a humble representative of God in this world.

HOW DOES MY SOUL EXPRESS ITSELF IN JEWISH LIFE?

Just as the physical body needs the soul to be alive, so too, the soul needs the physical body to connect to this world and express itself. The soul expresses itself through what are referred to as *levushim* garments. There are three levushim: *Machshava* (thought), *Dibur* (speech) and *Maaseh* (action). When we think, speak and do positive actions, we elevate our soul. Although one would think that accessing something spiritual should be through more mystical channels, there truly is a very accessible and practical way to elevate our soul. When making use of the levushim, they become an expression of the soul, much like clothing expresses a message of the person wearing them. The

SPEECH

ACTION

combinations of thought, speech and action required to observe the commandments are the levushim that together clothe the whole soul. Just as each commandment is associated with a limb and bone in our body, the commandments serve as levushim related to each part of our soul.

The *Tanya* teaches us that the levushim are on a higher level than our souls because the Torah and *mitzvot* are one with God. Therefore, when we wear them through learning and the performance of mitzvot, the soul is enabled to rise to a very high spiritual level. [1]

1 Tanya Chapter 4

THE ULTIMATE LEVUSH

The ultimate levush is the study of Torah, which involves both thought and speech. Torah is considered to be the thoughts of God, and through its study, we are given the most direct connection to Him. On the one hand, we wrap our thoughts and speech around the concepts and laws of the Torah, while on the other hand, we immerse ourselves in Torah, so it wraps itself around us. This creates an intimate connection with God that no other mitzvah provides.

WHAT HAPPENS TO MY SOUL WHEN I DIE?

Upon death, our Divine soul returns to God, its creator. Based on our behavior in this world, a judgment is made before a Heavenly court. All the positive and negative actions are presented like a movie of our lives. Watching the movie can be very shocking seeing who you really are and how much of your true purpose and potential you fulfilled. On the other hand, it can be very pleasurable seeing all that you achieved in your sincere service of God and your fellow man in the way you were meant to do so.

The Heavenly court will also ask us questions such as, "Were your business dealings faithful?" and, "Did you set fixed times for Torah study?" and, "Did you engage in procreation?" Before being rewarded for all the good we do, most of us have to experience some level of cleansing of any spiritual stains caused by our misdeeds for which we did not repent during our lifetime. This purification is referred to as *Gehinom*, which can last from a short period to a full twelve-month process, depending on the severity of the sins one has taken with them to the next world. Most people receive less, which is why mourners, *kaddish* is only said for eleven months.

After the purification process, the Divine soul enjoys the spiritual pleasure of a closeness to God without any of the distractions caused by the animal soul. This will continue until after the coming of Mashiach, when the world will enter into a spiritual state of Olam Haba, the world to come, which is similar to the Garden of Eden. The pleasure of such spiritual bliss is beyond our comprehension. The soul dwells in a world close to God without any of the Klipas of life in this world. Eventually, we will experience the revival of the dead when all purified souls will be reunited with our bodies that also went through the purification process by being buried in the "dust of the earth" from which we were originally created. The physical world will then be elevated where we can experience pure spirituality within the physical world.

IN CONCUSION

Dear Reader,

I hope that the visual and descriptive "pictures of the soul" have helped you gain a better understanding of who you are and what to strive toward in your life. I hope that this book has helped make your soul a more tangible reality within your conscious mind and in your heart. I also hope that you have gained a greater ability to distinguish between the voices of your animal soul from those of your Divine soul and that you can develop the ammunition to become increasingly victorious in the inner battle. Remember that God is on your side. Both contemplation and awakening His hidden love for you should become a part of your daily life so that your love of God and love for yourself should continue to grow. Using the wisdom of our sages to understand how your mind operates should make you more productive in every area of life. Take the time to learn Torah and attend classes that build your soul awareness in order to keep your mind inspired and more and more connected to God who loves you and wants to see you succeed and live a truly happy life.

Feel free to contact me at david@realyouproject.com

Enjoy my other works www.realyouproject.com

Sincerely,

David

The soul (Neshama) of man is a candle of God.

MISHLEI 20:27

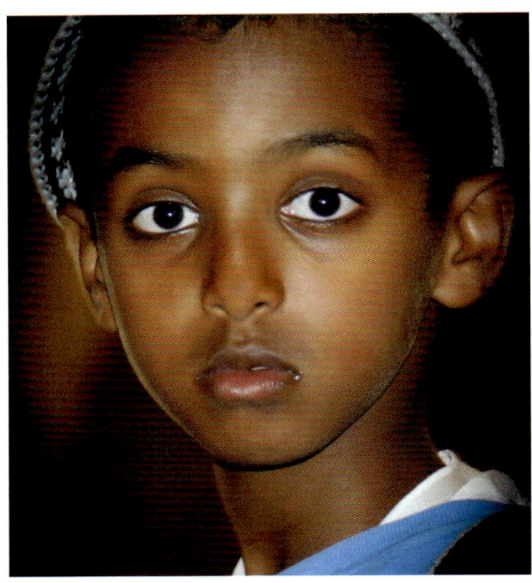

Being aware of the piece of divinity within you can dramatically change the way you perceive yourself and the way others perceive you.

We must try to always remember that the Divine essence of who we are is purely holy.